GROWING AND DECORATING WITH GRASSES

Also by H. PETER LOEWER

The Indoor Water Gardener's How-To Handbook
Bringing the Outdoors In
Seeds and Cuttings

GROWING AND DECORATING WITH GRASSES

WRITTEN AND ILLUSTRATED BY

H. Peter Loewer

WALKER AND COMPANY • New York

First published in the United States of America in 1977 by the Walker Publishing Company, Inc.
Published simultaneously in Canada by Fitzhenry & Whiteside, Limited, Toronto

Cloth bound ISBN: 0-8027-0562-6
Paperback ISBN: 0-8027-7112-2

Library of Congress Catalog Card Number: 76-53640

Printed in the United States of America

Book design by Robert Barto

10 9 8 7 6 5 4 3 2 1

Contents

List of Plants Illustrated

LIST OF ADDITIONAL ILLUSTRATIONS

ALL FLESH IS GRASS, AND ALL THE GOODLINESS THEREOF IS
AS THE FLOWER OF THE FIELD . . .

—ISAIAH 40:6

Preface

A wan, winter sun is shining today, its weak rays bouncing with a lackluster brilliance on endless fields and forests of extremely cold, cold snow; for this is the infamous "Winter of 77," and I, and a vast majority of fellow citizens, am sick with cold. My greenhouse has two blooming orchids, three pots of miniature cyclamen, a Rieger begonia, and an assortment of house plants that have become close friends through the years; it also has one clay pot of Cloud Grass (*Agrostis nebulosa*) that I've been growing in order to draw the blossoms for this book (my initial planting was consumed last fall by a herd of hungry deer). That one pot of grass, glowing with the bright, vivid green that only springtime can usually produce, is a truly wondrous sight on a day like today.

My pot of Cloud Grass is one of over one hundred grasses that I've grown over the past two years in order to compile the information and drawings for this book. Books on ornamental grasses are few and far between, which is evident from my bibliography. I've never enjoyed exploring a family of plants more and only hope that the reader will become as enthusiastic as I. I would appreciate hearing from any readers who have information or knowledge of grasses not covered in this book, as I know there are many more unknown to me. (Just last week, I was introduced to some miniature grasses found in the Himalayas.) Send all communications to me at Walker and Company, 720 Fifth Avenue, New York, N.Y. 10019.

As in the past, I owe a debt of gratitude to my publisher, Mr. Samuel Walker, for originally asking me to do this book; my editor, Mr. Richard Winslow, for his continuing support and aid in seeing both the forest and the trees; my wife, Jean, for her mental encouragement and physical help in the nurture and reaping of the grasses themselves; and finally the many nurserymen, who have aided me in finding all the seeds and plants necessary to make this expedition into a new world of gardening.

Introduction

The grasses, *Graminaeae* to the botanist, represent the most important single plant family on earth, since they alone produce all the cereal grains that have sustained humanity throughout recorded history. Corn, wheat, rice, oats, barley, rye, sorghum, cane sugar, and the bamboos are all close plant relations. They store in their seeds and/or foliage the vitamins, starches, sugars, and other nourishment that makes these plants more valuable to mankind than all others combined.

This book deals with a very small segment of the over 10,000 cataloged species: those grown for ornament in home and garden. Popular in Europe and Asia for hundreds of years, the ornamental grasses have been largely overlooked by the American gardener in favor of plants that are thought to be showier in form and color. If the American public knows the ornamental grasses at all, it's as dried accompaniment to winter bouquets.

There are, perhaps, more than a few reasons for this oversight. Most of the world's other cultures still maintain some contact with the land, and the concept of gardening—whether as food for the body or the soul—has a long and well-documented tradition. I have a book on floral engravings that shows Feather Grass (then called *Gramen Plumeum* and now termed *Stipa pennata*) as a decorative garden addition in Holland around the year 1696.* Today, in England and Europe, most of the population garden in one way or another, and house plants have been in vogue since the invention of the first "orangeries" or greenhouses in Jane Austen's time. Remember that life in a European coal or industrial slum was at best a drab and dismal existence, and people naturally turned to plants for what little color they could bring into their lives. This exposure to plants has led, over the years, to a greater sophistication on the part of the European gardener.

In Japan and China, where gardens have been appreciated for thousands of years, it is no longer important how many plant varieties one can grow, but rather how many facets one can see in a single plant. Theirs is a culture that finds restful contemplation in gardens made entirely of mosses, grasses, or stones; not only does one enjoy a flower, but in turn, the stem, the leaf, the entire plant, and even the shadow it casts upon a garden wall.

Today, our culture is a mobile one, and because of economic demands, either real or imagined, the typical family no longer settles in one place for its entire existence, and few people bother with the less flamboyant or slower growing members of the plant world. Instead, we demand the fast tree and the blatant bloom, and thus the graceful grasses are relegated to the lawn for

*Abraham Munting, *Decorative Floral Engravings*, ed. Theodore Menten (New York: Dover Publications, 1975), p. 84.

cutting and the gift shops of colonial Williamsburg, where as dried flowers, they remind us of our agricultural past.

At this point I'm reminded of two memories: the first was my initial glimpse of a mature clump of Zebra Grass in Paula Roos's twenty-year-old suburban garden in Honesdale, Pennsylvania, and the sheer grace and majesty it commanded; the second is the following story of two American visitors touring an English estate:

"Goodness," said the wife as she trod the palatial lawn, "this grass is beautiful," and turning to the head gardener asked: "How do you get a beautiful lawn like this?"

"Well, ma'am, first you roll it for about four hundred years," he replied.

Chapter one explains the structure of the grasses and the functioning of their parts, including the flowers and seeds, why they have been so successful as plants, and why some varieties spell trouble in a manicured lawn.

Chapter two covers the annual grasses, those that germinate, bloom, seed, and die in one growing season. These annuals, like Bearded Wheat and Quaking Grass, are ideal as cut flowers, both fresh and dried, and their feathery sprays should be found in all annual flower beds. I have labeled them Hardy, Half-Hardy, and Tender, based on their ability to survive low and freezing temperatures.

Chapter three deals with the larger, perennial species of grass, like Zebra Grass and Maiden Grass, that flourish in the garden for many years, forming larger and larger clumps. I've considered a grass a perennial if it will survive a winter where temperatures fall to below 32°F. (A table to convert Fahrenheit to Celsius is found in Appendix D for the convenience of those who want to plunge into the metric world.) While many perennials, when dried or cut, make marvelous displays indoors, they are generally grown in the home landscape for their attractive foliage. In addition, I've included as perennials several tropical species that have been enjoyed as house plants over the years.

Chapter four covers sedges and rushes, including some fascinating history of the rush. These are the plants that greatly resemble grasses, but upon closer examination, they differ in structure, and often, habit.

Chapter five concerns those plants that at first glance are thought to be grasses, like Blue-Eyed Grass, but with a closer look and armed with a bit of botanical knowledge are found to be from entirely different families.

Chapter six is devoted to the bamboos, plants that have a grand and versatile tradition in the Orient but are relatively new to the American gardener, both outdoors and in.

Chapter seven gives instructions on drying the grasses for winter bouquets and also covers other uses for interior decoration, including some sage advice from over one hundred years ago.

The appendixes include a list of a number of reputable firms that supply both seeds and/or living plants of the ornamental grasses. It is by no means a complete list, as I'm sure to have missed many more nurseries. I have also included a few organizations that will, on occasion, cover many species of grass either in their publications or seed exchanges. I received my 1977 seeds from the Alpine Garden Society, and they include two wild fescues and an unnamed species of *Melica* grass from the Zagros Mountains of Iran.

Missing from this book is a map of climate zones. Such maps are very general, at best, and usually difficult to pin down. Instead is the following table of temperatures; just look for the lowest experienced in your vicinity.

Approximate Range of Average Annual Minimum Temperatures (Fahrenheit) for Each Zone

Zone 1	below -50°		
Zone 2	-50°	to	-40°
Zone 3	-40°	to	-30°
Zone 4	-30°	to	-20°
Zone 5	-20°	to	-10°
Zone 6	-10°	to	0°
Zone 7	0°	to	10°
Zone 8	10°	to	20°
Zone 9	20°	to	30°
Zone 10	30°	to	40°

The wind-chill factor chart in Appendix D should be used in conjunction with the above.

The bibliography is annotated.

A Word or Two on Nomenclature

Just as I was finishing the illustrations for this book, the long-awaited publishing event of the botanical world burst upon the scene with the arrival of *Hortus III* (see the bibliography). As a result, many of the plants described have been given their new Latin names and, as a result, lost the old. Since *Hortus* is the definitive guide on scientific names, most of the plant and seed suppliers will change their catalogs in a reasonably short time and will then match the names in this book. Although it is true that many grasses can be recognized by their common name, it is absolutely mandatory to use the scientific name when you are inquiring about or buying plants, both here and abroad, to be sure that you and your correspondent are talking about the same thing.

The first thing to remember is that all plants known to man have been given Latin names. In the 1700s when the present system of classification began, Latin was the international language of scholars, and thus it was the obvious language to use.

The three terms in general use are: *genus, species*, and *variety* or, gaining in usage, *cultivar*. In print, the *genus* and *species* are always set off from the accompanying text, usually by use of *italics*. The *genus* is always capitalized. When used, the *variety* is also *italicized* and usually preceded by the abbreviation "var." in roman type. Plants previously classified often had varietal names that recorded a change in the parent plant, either by accident or design, that showed up in succeeding generations. This is now termed "cultivar" and is designated by roman type set off by single quotation marks or set in a completely different typeface and capitalized.

Thus, Bulbous Oat Grass is termed *Arrhenatherum* (genus), *elatius (species)*, var. (variety as previously classified) *bulbosum*, 'Variegatum' (cultivar). Since I never had the benefit of Latin in my education, I've wondered for years about the different endings on words after the species, especially variegatum, variegatus, and variegata. The answer, I discover, is that all the words in the name must reflect the same endings, thus: *Acorus gramineus variegatus* and *Arundinaria Simonii* var. *variegata*. Also, note that the species names are capitalized when they are derived from the names of persons and places.

On Importing Plants from Overseas and the U.S.D.A.

When I was deeply involved in writing this book, I found that one of the best sources for the more unusual ornamental grasses is England, notably

Hilliers & Sons in Winchester (see Appendix A). As you know, the United States is ever vigilant in guarding against imported pests (remember the Japanese Beetle?), and all plants imported from foreign countries are closely watched for insects or disease. If you wish to import plants, you must have an *Import Permit for Plants and Plant Products* that assigns you a registration number and Permit Stamps that *you* must send to the seller along with each order. These stamps advise the seller that unless the plants are washed clean of soil and packed in a sterile medium like sphagnum moss, they will not be allowed into the United States. Although, as with any government activity, it takes time to get a permit, the service is free. Just write to:

United States Department of Agriculture
Animal and Plant Health Inspection Service
Plant Protection and Quarantine Programs
Federal Center Building
Hyattsville, Maryland 20782

The forms make the procedure look a bit complicated, but it really isn't, and most nurseries in Europe are quite familiar with the procedure. Remember to allow time for the shipments, and try to place your order in early spring in the northeast, before the docks of Hoboken, New Jersey, swelter with summer heat and fry your plant.

Receiving plants (and seeds) from another country by mail is the next best thing to traveling in person.

The Botany of Grass

GO TO GRASS!

—Beaumont and Fletcher, *Knight of the Burning Pestle*

The Concise Oxford Dictionary, fifth edition, defines *grass* as "Herbage of which blades or leaves and stalks are eaten by cattle, horses, sheep, etc. . . . any species of this (including in botanical use, excluding in popular use) the cereals, reeds, and bamboos . . ." which is probably as good a definition as any other. For meanings of grass that are further afield, we have the following: never let *grass* grow under one's feet; turn out to *grass* (which is a deplorable habit of American civilization); a *grass* widow, which once referred to the actual state of widowhood (and, I'm sure we have *grass* widowers); go to *grass*! (which is a fairly polite way of telling someone off); keep off the *grass*; *grass* doesn't grow on a busy street; *grass* colt, which refers to a colt with an unknown parentage, and a slang way of saying the same of people; bring to *grass* (an English term that refers to shooting an animal or bird); and finally the term made so popular during the 60s: *grass.*

Beyond the impact of grass on the origin and use of words, the grasses are endlessly beautiful plants represented by over 1,400 naturally occurring species in the United States alone. Grasses run the gamut from the 120-foot Giant Bamboo (*Dendrocalamus giganteus*) to the tiny Dwarf Fescues (*Festuca* spp.), only a few inches high. We're all familiar with the food grasses and their grains (corn, wheat, etc.), but most domestic animals, and many in the wild, depend on the forage grasses that produce hay (Timothy, *Phleum pratense*),the pasture grasses represented by the Little Bluestem (*Schizachyrium scoparium*) and the Big Bluestem (*Andropogon Gerardi*), and the silage grasses, mostly corn and sorghum.

Bamboos are used all over the Orient for scaffolding in construction, water pipes, cooking utensils, food, art objects, and as decorative garden and house plants. Grasses are also used to fight erosion. Vast stretches of American beaches have been planted with American Beachgrass (*Ammophila breviligulata*), since its tight, fibrous root system digs in and actually holds sand from blowing away. The *Spartinas* and *Phragmites* perform the same service for the coastal wetlands and shallow marshes. The ground around your house would wash away without a grass cover, and playing golf on a sand course would be unthinkable.

Besides lichens and algae, the grasses are the only other plants found in the remotest polar regions and the hottest deserts of the world. The next time you pass a construction site, where the worst soil imaginable has been piled up next to a stagnant pool, look for grass, and chances are you'll find a few plants starting to come up. Their ability to withstand prolonged periods of drought, to form extensive mats of growth with their knack of rooting along the stem at nodes, their dependence on the wind for pollination rather than insects, and efficient seed production and dispersal have given the grasses an

A+ mark on the evolutionary report card and a greater range around the world than any other plant family. Contrary to popular belief, all grasses do not look alike! And once their structures are understood, the different groups are easy to identify.

The *stems* or *culms* (1) of grasses are usually round and hollow, as in wheat *(Triticum* spp*.)*, but sometimes they have solid stems, as in corn *(Zea mays)*, or where a species has survived in very arid regions. The stem sections are joined by solid joints or *nodes* (2). These stems may stand erect like the great fields of wheat or corn, or bend at the joints as many of the Panic Grasses do, or trail along the surface of the soil like Crab Grass, in which case the stems become *stolons* (3). When the stolons continue to grow just beneath the surface of the ground, they are termed *rhizomes* (4), and the growth of these rhizomes is a method of reproducing which is almost as effective as seeds, amply demonstrated by the ability of your lawn, and the weedy grasses in it, to spread. The *root* systems are very fibrous (5) and many types of grass have roots that penetrate the earth for many feet, straight down. It is this quality that makes the grasses so valuable in erosion control and also prevents you from completely removing an unwanted grass without a good deal of hard digging. The great prairies of America were once covered with vast areas of grasses that would burn every year in awesome prairie fires; yet come spring the grasses would renew themselves. Here in the east, field fires are very common and are often used to clear the land. But the grasses grow again because the root systems go so deeply that they are protected from the heat. This also saves the grasses from undue damage by drought.

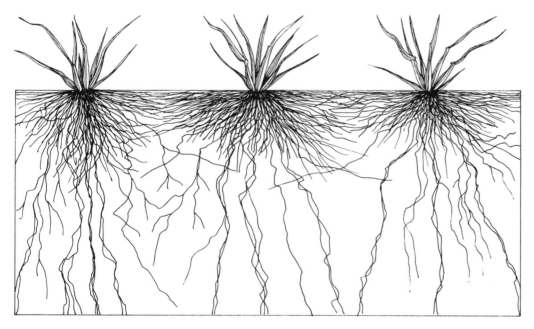

The leaves are always parallel-veined and belong to the great group of plants known as the *monocotyledones*, easily identified by grass seedlings that always begin with one seed leaf.* The leaves consist of a *blade* (6) and a *sheath* (7) that surrounds the culm. Where the blade meets the sheath, a small hairy collar is usually found. This is termed the *ligule* (8) and is a distinguishing characteristic of grasses (in English: "little tongue").

---

*There are two great subdivisions of flowering plants: the *monocotyledons* and the *dicotyledons*. Dicotyledons generally have leaves with a complex shape, such as maples, and young seedlings have two leaves. Monocotyledons have simpler leaf shapes and from a standpoint of evolution are considered to be the more advanced form, working on the theory that less is best.

Since most of the grasses depend on the wind for pollination, they have no need for extensive and magnificent floral displays; garish petals and nectars attract bees, ants, beetles, and birds to do the job of pollination. The grasses cast their pollen out to float from flower to flower on gentle breezes. The flower parts are essentially the same as those of other plants, but a few features, like petals, have all but disappeared, and the rest are so small that they should be seen with a magnifying glass. The *lemma* (9), which in turn gives rise to another major feature of the grasses, the *awn* (10); the *palea* (11), and the *lodicule* (12), are but the remains of the petals of a typical flower. The *stamens* (13) are male; and the *stigma* (14)—usually plumed to aid in picking pollen out of the air—is female and surmounts the *ovary* (15), where seeds are produced.

The flower clusters (or inflorescence) are made up of subdivisions called *spikelets* (16) and are usually *perfect*, meaning both male and female parts are found within the same bloom. The spikelets are arranged in three different forms: the *terminal spike* (17) as in Foxtail Grass, a *panicle* as in Orchard Grass (18), and *reacemes* as in Common Manna Grass (19).

Many grasses flower with such precise timing that a watch could be set by their blooming habits. The brizias open about 6:00 A.M., the bromes at 2:00 P.M., and the avenas start at about 3:00 P.M. The process begins when the lemma and palea start to open, allowing the anthers to spread and shake their pollen on the wind; the feathery stigmas are now ready to receive pollen from other flowers. Grasses rarely self-fertilize; they usually are sterile to their own pollen.

The seeds of the grasses assume many sizes and shapes, all readily adapted to dispersal by animal, including man, but generally by the wind. Many of the bromes have barbed tips that easily penetrate the hair of animals or clothes of man, and often the awns twitch with changes in the humidity and drive the tips directly into an animal's skin. Others are less harmful, exhibiting long and attractive plumes that float them through the air in the same manner as dandelion fluff. Man, too, has been an active agent in the spread of grasses, and many African grasses that were used for bedding in slave ships (e.g. Bermuda Grass and Molasses Grass) followed along and began to grow at all ports-of-call. Seeds have frequently come into the country as impurities in other seed mixes or in grain shipments.

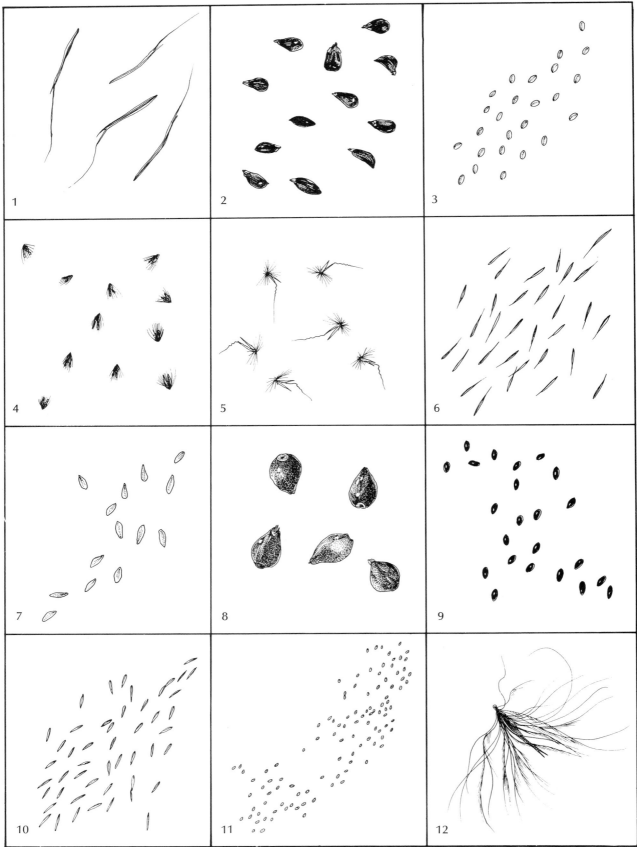

The accompanying illustration shows the seeds of twelve grasses at about their natural size:
(1) *Bromus madrintensis,* **(2)** Strawberry Corn, **(3)** *Setaria glauca,* **(4)** Champagne Grass, **(5)** Zebra Grass, **(6)** *Festuca glauca,* **(7)** Canary Grass, **(8)** Job's Tears **(9)** Black Sorghum, **(10)** *Koeleria glauca,* **(11)** *Eragrostis tef,* **(12)** *Pennisetum longistylum.*

# The Annual Grasses

SPREADING HERE, SPREADING THERE, THE GRASSES ON THE PLAIN,
A CYCLE, A YEAR OF FLOURISHING AND DECAY . . .
—Po Chü-Yi, *A Song of Farewell*

The annual grasses, as a group, are rarely grown for their foliage, which, at best, looks weedy. But the flowers and seeds of the annuals offer so many fascinating varieties of form—and color—that one never ceases to admire this output of Nature.

A few of the annuals demand a prominent position in the garden bed and border, as the plants themselves are small and the flowers large, like Golden Top. Others are best confined to that old-fashioned standby—the cutting garden—where they can be gathered at the proper time (as I will indicate) and dried for winter ornamentation. Remember too, that seed should be collected then for use the following season. Since none of these grasses are hybrids, they will grow true to seed. Store all the seed in carefully marked packages in a cool, dry place.

As a general rule, the annual grasses require a position with full summer sun* for adequate growth and flowering, but are not too fussy about soil conditions. In order to have a sequence of bloom throughout the summer, I always start some seeds indoors in early spring. It will take about 3-4 weeks for the seeds to germinate. Then give them plenty of light to prevent leggy growth. Many of the annual grasses are marketed by English and European firms, where the terms Hardy Annuals, Half-Hardy Annuals, and Tender Annuals are more likely to be used than in the United States. I think they are very handy terms if one lives in a climate like mine, where frosts can persist well into June, and where many years we feel blessed if we have ninety consecutive days without a freeze. Hardy Annuals (HA) seed can be planted directly out-of-doors at any time the ground is workable; Half-Hardys (HHA) can withstand some degree of cold, but not too much; and the Tender Annuals (TA) must wait until all chance of frost is past.

Caution: When planting annual grass seeds directly out-of-doors, prepare and mark the seed bed with care; the new little plants look for all the world like any other grassy weed leading to ultimate confusion and dismay. I was careless last year and lost much of my Hare's-tail Grass, which was squeezed out by a local Panic Grass, before I realized what was happening. When seedlings are one to two inches tall, thin them out six to twelve inches between each plant, depending on their ultimate height: Wild Oats, for example, should be one foot apart, while the Hare's-tail only needs a six-inch space. Also, be generous with the seed, as the smaller grasses look much better when planted in substantial groupings of the same species.

---

* For growing grasses indoors, see Chapter six.

Cloud Grass, *Agrostis nebulosa* (HA), 8-20 inches tall.
This lovely grass is native to the Iberian Peninsula, and while it has many North American relatives, none are quite as delicate and cloudlike in total effect. A border of these plants makes a beautiful sight, although the plants never last very long, dying soon after they flower. This is one of the few annuals that can take a position in partial shade and still look and flower well.

Since the plants are fairly small, try a potful indoors while the snow is still on the ground; just give the plants plenty of light.

The panicles can be carefully picked and dried, and make a valuable addition to winter arrangements.

Wild Oats, *Avena fatua* (HA), 3-4 feet tall.
Most eastern farmers consider this a weed, and it can be found along many roadsides in high summer. The plant is straggly looking, even for a grass, but the flowers are most attractive and have a beautiful shade of light brown. It quickly goes to seed and dies, so the flowers should be picked early.

Animated Oats, *Avena sterilis* (HA), 3-4 feet tall.
This grass is a larger version of the Wild Oats and originally comes from Europe. It, too, is unattractive at best, but the flowers are excellent for winter bouquets. The common name comes from the movement of the awns as the atmospheric humidity changes. It is an excellent grass flower to examine, as all the parts are large enough to view with ease. The plants really do best with full sun, and the seeds will germinate within ten days.

Quaking Grass, *Briza maxima* (HHA), 2-3 feet tall.
Native to Southern Europe, Quaking Grass has been in cultivation as a garden ornament for well over 200 years. The spikelets quiver and quake with every gentle movement of the breeze and look a lot like the popular cereal that was "shot from guns" when I was young. In addition, the lemmas are faintly striped with purple, making this a most attractive addition to any bouquet. It should be limited to the cutting garden, as it's too ungainly for a prominent spot elsewhere. The seeds will germinate in 10-14 days and are easily started in peat pots in early spring. The panicles should be picked before they open.

Little Quaking Grass, *Briza minor* (HHA), 6-18 inches tall.
If the epithet "cute" can be correctly applied to a grass, this one is it. A miniature of Quaking Grass, the same general rules for growing it apply, except that heavy summer rains can quickly smash the plants. Show the flowers to people alongside the larger relative, and tell them you've invented a secret shrinking process, and they just might believe you.

Brome Grass, *Bromus macrostachys* (HA), 18-24 inches tall.
Originally found in Southern Europe, the Brome Grasses have many North American relatives, called Chess or Cheat Grasses. While again not too good for an upfront position in the garden, the flowers retain all their character when dried. They need full sun and should be sown outdoors in spring.

Brome Grass, *Bromus madritensis* (HA), 18-24 inches tall.
Another of the Brome family. The same growing conditions as the previous example, and another beautiful addition to dried bouquets.

Cloud Grass
Agrostis nebulosa

Animated Oats
Avena sterilis

Wild Oats
Avena fatua

Little Quaking Grass
Briza minor

Quaking Grass
Briza maxima

3

2

1

0

Brome Grass
Bromus macrostachys

Brome Grass
Bromus madritensis

2

1

0

Job's Tears, *Coix Lacryma-Jobi* (HHA), 3-4 feet tall.
A close relative of the corns, Job's Tears has the distinction of being one of the oldest ornamental grasses in cultivation. It is said to have been used in the fourteenth century. The seeds readily fall from the plant at maturity and are hard, white, streaked with gray or black, and very shiny. For years the seeds have been used for jewelry, especially rosaries, and the plants are often found growing wild in the southern states. The beads are the female flower and bear two feathery stigmas and two green male flowers above.

Job's Tears will tolerate some shade and a damp spot in the garden. The leaves are an attractive, light green. In colder climate, start the seeds indoors in individual peat pots. Three to four weeks are required for germination.

A form with variegated leaves, *C. Lacryma-Jobi* var. *zebrina*, is sometimes available if you search.

Love Grass, *Eragrostis tef* (TA), 18-24 inches tall.
This grass, once called *Eragrostis abyssinica,* and in Ethiopia called Tef, is one of the many Love Grasses cultivated in gardens. It has been grown in India and Australia for a forage plant, and in Africa the seeds are still ground for flour and used in breadmaking. Give the plants plenty of sun, and don't put them out until all danger of frost is past. An American species, *E. capillaris*, or Lace Grass, is a more open version of Tef and is often found growing on the borderline between fields and woods in the Northeast. Others of this tribe are mentioned in the perennial section.

Hare's-tail Grass, *Lagurus ovatus* (HA), 18-24 inches tall.
Here is another native Mediterranean grass, in cultivation for years and naturalized in parts of England. Hare's-tail Grass is the only species in the genus. The name in Greek is *lagos*, a hare, and *oura*, a tail. It's a lovely grass and produces a great many terminal spikes by the time of the killing frost. The foliage is light green, and the stems and leaves are soft with down. It is widely used in winter bouquets.

Besides being attractive, the flower heads do not shatter with age. It is also widely mistreated by people who feel the absolute necessity to continually improve on nature and dye the seed heads electric pink, or liver green, or malaria yellow, and then place them in plastic vases to be sold to the weary driver at interstate and thruway rest-stops.

Golden Top, *Lamarkia aurea* (TA), 18-24 inches tall.
Named after J. B. Lamarck, the naturalist who lost out to Darwin in the evolutionary sweepstakes, Golden Top is truly a unique and beautiful grass. If I had to limit my choice of annual grasses to one, this would be it. The one-sided panicles have a shimmering golden effect when fresh that becomes silvery with age. By mid-summer, the plants are turning brown, so a second crop should be prepared. The flowers shatter easily when dry, so be sure and pick them before they mature. Golden Top occurs as a weed in the southwestern states.

Feather Top Grass, *Pennisetum villosum*, 2-3 feet tall.
Although this grass from Ethiopia is a perennial in Zone 9, most catalogs list it as a Half-Hardy Annual, where in addition it is often listed as *Pennisetum longistylum*. Feather Top is rather floppy in appearance, for the magnificent flowers become quite heavy. If picked before they open entirely, they can be dried for bouquets but readily shatter with the slightest bump. They're beautiful when picked as fresh flowers and surrounded with Garden Phlox, or Coral Bells and Astilbe. The seeds should be planted out-of-doors when all danger of frost is past.

Job's Tears
Coix Lacryma-Jobi

4
3
2
1
0

Love Grass
Eragrostis tef

2

1

0

Hare's-tail Grass
Lagurus ovatus

Golden Top
Lamarkia aurea

2

1

0

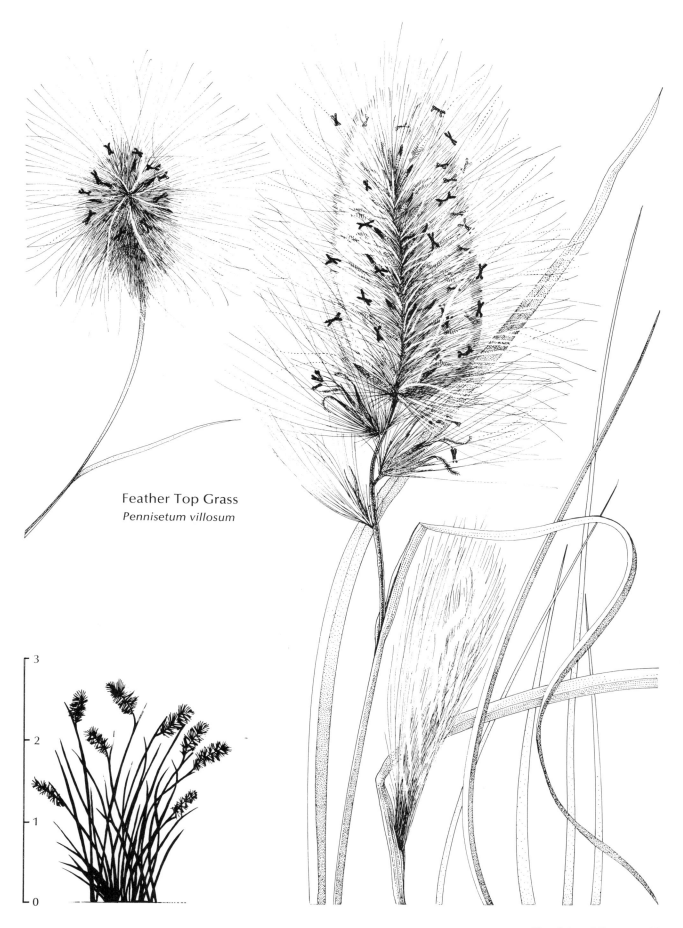

Feather Top Grass
Pennisetum villosum

3

2

1

0

Canary Grass, *Phalaris canariensis* (HA), 2-3 feet tall.
This grass is native to the Canary Islands and Southern Europe and is birdseed for both wild and domesticated canaries. The flower-heads are a variegated green and yellowish-white at the top of long slender stems. While the plant itself is not attractive enough to win a spot in the flower garden, it is a good choice for dried bouquets. Since bird-cage bottoms often go to landfills, Canary Grass is often seen at the town dump. A perennial relative, *Phalaris arundinacea* var. *picta,* will be mentioned in that section.

Champagne Grass, *Rhynchelytrum repens*, 3-4 feet tall.
Also known as *Rhynchelytrum roseum* and *Tricholaena rosea*, in addition to Ruby Grass and Natal Grass. This is my second favorite annual grass. It is another plant that's listed as a Half-Hardy Annual in the catalogs, while being a perennial in Zone 9. It blooms over a long season, only to be cut down by frost, when the reddish-pink plumes turn to a soft silver. While it is a great freshly cut flower and easily shatters with age, you can dry it for indoor bouquets if it isn't knocked about too much. When gathering, pull the stems out of the leaf sheath, rather than break them.

Foxtail Millet, *Setaria italica* (HA), 2-4 feet tall.
This is a striking annual grass that really looks like a foxtail that was tied on the rumble seat of an old Chevie during the 30s. The dense panicles are often up to a foot in length and bow toward the earth with the weight of the seed grains. While the plants are tolerant to some lack of water, they perish quickly under drought conditions. First grown in Ancient China 2700 B.C., Foxtail reached Europe during the Middle Ages, and in 1849 entered the United States, where it has become an important fodder crop. The seed is harvested for bird feed. This is another grass that is a bit too ungainly for a formal garden, but the panicles are striking additions to winter decorations and last as long as you have the patience to dust them.

Foxtail Grass, *Setaria lutescens* (HA), 18-24 inches tall.
Often called *Setaria glauca* in the catalogs, Foxtail Grass was originally a common weed in Europe, and, after its introduction, has become a common weed in America. The bristles of the panicles have a definite yellow-orange color that remains after drying and is very attractive. It is not fussy and should go into a cutting garden.

Black Sorghum, *Sorghum bicolor* var. *technicus* (HHA), 4-6 feet tall.
Widely cultivated since prehistoric times, the Sorghums have been used by man for many things: some produce molasses from their sweet juices; the grain from others is employed in making flour; a third type is grown specifically to manufacture brooms; and a fourth provides silage and fodder for cattle. I've grown Black Sorghum strictly for the garden. The shiny, black panicle spruces up any floral arrangement, and the leaves, with their light green color that's lightly spattered with brown, are very effective when used with cut flowers. Like Corn, give plenty of sunlight and never plant outside until all frosts are past.

Wheat, *Triticum aestivum* (HA), 3-4 feet tall.
Previously known as *Triticum spelta*, the cultivation of this cereal annual goes far back in time. It's extremely hardy but not very good for flour, so today it is used primarily for cattle. As an ornamental, the flowering stalks are very tall and the racemes most unusual with their regular order. A large group of these plants in a garden is a must. The seeds can be planted in early spring and will germinate in 5-10 days.

Canary Grass
Phalaris canariensis

3

2

1

0

Champagne Grass
Rhynchelytrum repens

Foxtail Millet

Foxtail Grass

Setaria lutescens

Setaria italica

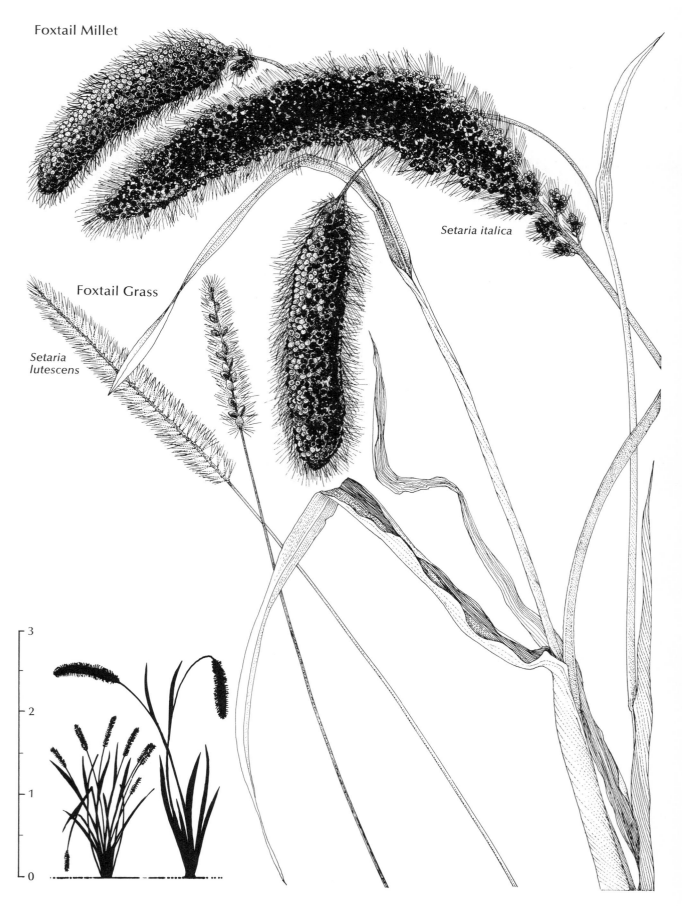

Black Sorghum

Sorghum bicolor var. technicus

Bearded Wheat
Triticum turgidum

Triticum aestivum

var. gracillima 'Variegata'

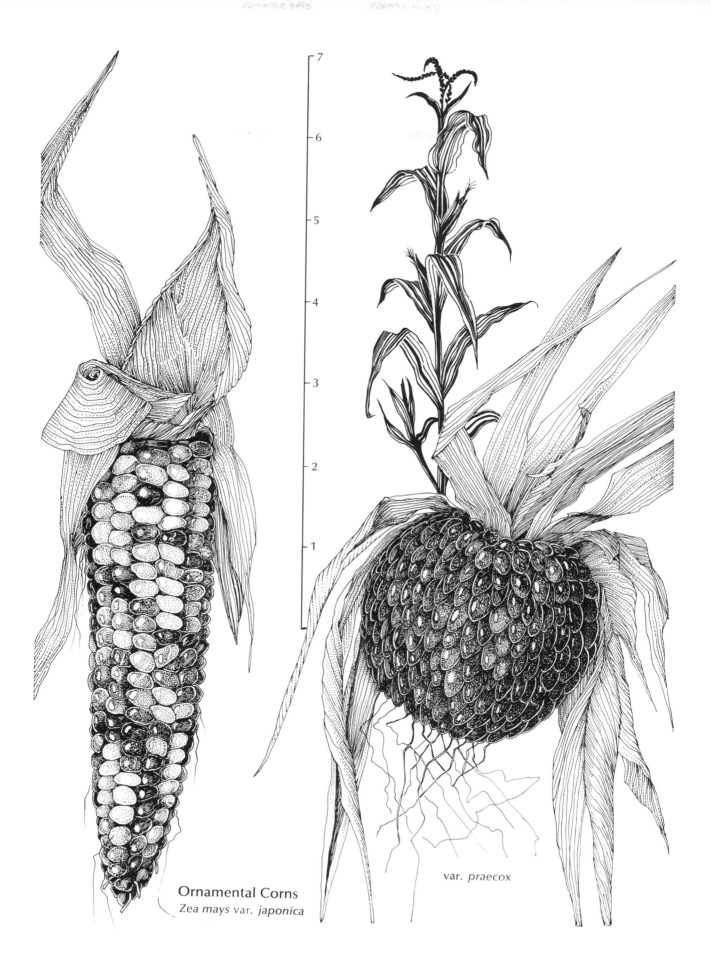

Ornamental Corns
Zea mays var. *japonica*

var. *praecox*

Bearded Wheat, *Triticum turgidum* (HA), 2-4 feet tall.
The flour from Bearded Wheat is known as Duram and is very popular for use in pasta flours. It is very hardy, drought resistant, and grown in most arid regions of the world. The long awns are unlike any other grass inflorescence, and a vase full of dried stalks is an attention-getter every time. The cultural instructions are the same as for Wheat.

Variegated Corn, *Zea mays* var. *gracillima* 'Variegata' (TA), 3-4 feet tall.
This is a relatively miniature Corn, and unlike most annual grasses, is grown for its beautifully shaded leaves that are striped with green and pure white. The cobs never grow very large, and the silk just adds more interest to the plants. Corn is a rank feeder, so always plant in fertile soil, planning to add more fertilizer at monthly intervals; it also likes plenty of water. Since corn is very sensitive to cold and takes a goodly time for development, start plants indoors in individual "Jiffy-7's" or peat pots, transplanting as they grow. Try putting Variegated Corn in eight-inch pots, and group a few for a very effective outdoor-terrace decoration.

Zea mays var. *japonica* has the added distinction of a touch of red or pink with the variegations. There are other varieties of Corn listed in the trade as Rainbow Corn that produce ears of many-colored kernels. Strawberry Corn (var. *praecox*) grows roundish ears of pointed red kernels that are said to make very good popcorn.

Wild Rice, *Zizania aquatica* (HA), 6-8 feet tall.
Wild Rice today is an epicurian delight and very, very expensive when purchased by the quarter-pound package. It grows in the wild along inland marshes and at pond or lake edge mainly in northern Minnesota and Wisconsin. This grain was a major source of food for American Indian tribes before the modern age.

The plant itself is large and attractive in a waterside setting. Even a small pool may boast a few plants. Put them in pots with well-fertilized soil, covering the soil surface with gravel and submerging at the pool's edge. If you are lucky enough to have a stream or pond in a sunny position, be sure to try a grouping of Wild Rice, if not for your table, at least for the visiting waterfowl.

The small hanging spikelets on the bottom of the panicles are the male flowers, which eventually fall, leaving the rice-grains or female spikelets on the upper part.

The panicles can be gathered for bouquets but will shatter easily.

There are many other annual ornamental grasses in addition to those I've described. They include: Hair Grass (*Aira elegans*), Spike Grass (*Desmazeria sicula*), Dense Silky Bent Grass (*Apera interrupta*), Loose Silky Bent Grass (*Apera spica-venti*), Rabbit's-foot Grass (*Polypogon monspeliensis*), and another Love Grass (*Eragrostis tenella*). I'm sure there must be even more, but they will have to wait for another summer.

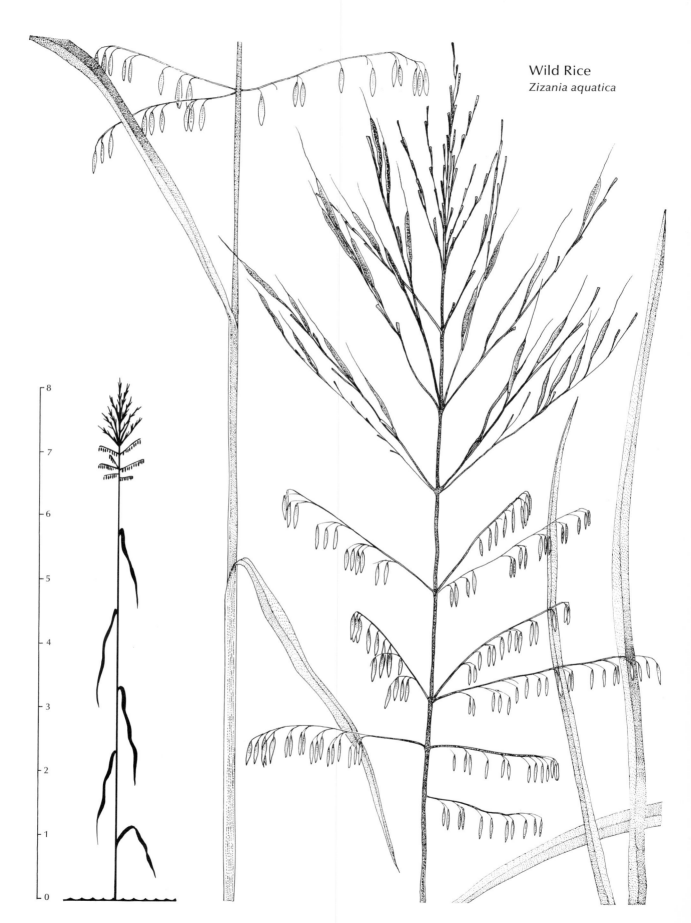

Wild Rice
Zizania aquatica

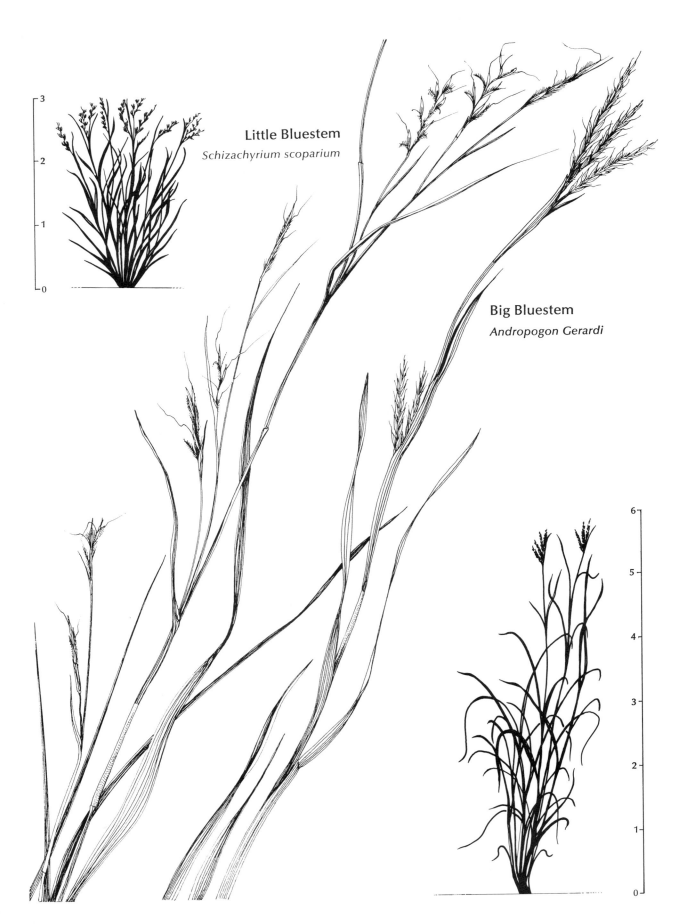

Little Bluestem
Schizachyrium scoparium

Big Bluestem
Andropogon Gerardi

3 The Perennial Grasses

BREATHLESS, WE FLUNG US ON THE WINDY HILL,
LAUGHED IN THE SUN, AND KISSED THE LOVELY GRASS.
—Rupert Brooke, *The Hill*

While many perennial grasses can be grown from seed, it's often faster (sometimes by two or three years) to buy established plants from nurseries. If you don't have a local source of supply, you can build up a complete collection ordering by mail. Even the United States Postal Service has not been able to completely destroy plants-by-mail, and United Parcel continues to be a big help. (Make sure that you allow plenty of time by ordering well in advance of the heat of your local summer. You can order in the fall for the following season.)

Your biggest concern in planning the perennial grasses is the final size of the plants. A mature clump of Zebra Grass *(Miscanthus sinensis* 'Zebrinus') is truly overwhelming. The young plant you purchased looked great under the kitchen window at the start, but now your kitchen is pitch dark, and you have trouble negotiating the car in the driveway! Consider the final size carefully, and, when planning your garden, consult the scale diagrams given with the drawings.

Most of the grasses prefer a fertile well-drained soil, generally in full sun. Any exceptions are noted in the cultural notes for each plant.

The only chore connected with the perennial grasses is the annual pruning of the larger types in early spring. That is the time to cut the dead stems and leaves to within 6 inches of the ground, before new growth begins. The larger clump-forming grasses grow from the inside out, and you may notice the plants are dead in the center after a few years. This is nothing to be upset about; it simply indicates that it's time to dig up the clumps and divide them. I'm sure you will have friends standing in line, waiting for a discarded plant. If the grass roots are too entangled for breaking with a shovel, you might have to divide the clump with an ax. Don't worry, these plants are not fragile and are very difficult to permanently damage. Unless the cultural discussion for each grass says differently, all the perennials can best be propagated by simple division of the rootstock.

Big Bluestem Grass, *Andropogon Gerardi* (USDA Zone 4), 4-6 feet tall.
This is one of America's great prairie grasses, robust and a favorite food of cattle. It's a native and called a "warm season grass" since it makes good pasture in the summer. The plants turn a beautiful shade of light reddish-brown after the first frost and persist on the landscape all winter long. The plants like water and are not as luxuriant when grown on poor and dry soil. If you use seed for prairie grasses, mark the plot well and be patient, since very little happens on the surface in the first year. Most of the plant's energy is spent sending down roots as long as ten feet. With such root systems, these grasses gain protection from excessive droughts and prairie fires. Many books

have been written on the establishment of the magnificent prairie grasses and their uses, which include low-maintenance lawns for those of you who are tired of cutting grass. Check the Appendix for the prairie-grass sources, and by all means read the book *Grass Lands* by the Wilsons, as it will introduce the East Coast and West Coast readers to another region of America that is endangered by the all-destroying bulldozer mentality.

Little Bluestem Grass, *Schizachyrium scoparium* (USDA Zone 4), 3-4 feet tall.
Until recently this grass was known as *Andropogon scoparius*, and while it is the state grass of Nebraska, it is found in forty-four other states. Like the Big Bluestem, this grass turns a golden reddish-brown in the fall. It is worth growing for that reason alone. You'll often find Little Blue in abandoned fields and along roadsides where it has been started for soil conservation. The flowers are small but very attractive when dried. It likes full sun and will get along on less water than Big Blue.

Bulbous Oat Grass, *Arrhenatherum elatius* var. *bulbosum* 'Variegatum'
(USDA Zone 5), 8-18 inches tall.
A white and green variegated leaf makes this a favorite garden grass. The name comes from the bulblike bottoms that are really swollen nodes on the stem. Each one of these "bulbs" will produce another plant, so you'll always have plenty on hand. In addition, the "bulbs" store water for the plant, making the plants sturdy in the face of drought. These are cool season grasses (unlike Big Bluestem) and do their best in spring and in the fall after the heat of mid-summer. In my cold climate, the leaves retain their shape and color well into December. The plants will take some shade but do their best in full sun.

Reed Grass, *Calamagrostis epigens* (USDA Zone 5), 3-4 feet tall.
When sick as a child, do you recall the security that came with the rustling sound of a nurse's skirts? Take my word for it, it's a comforting sound, and Reed Grass has the same effect when a light breeze blows upon its leaves. While often grown for its flowers, I find the leaves alone worth the effort. It grows well in wet or dry soil and will withstand some shade.

Northern Sea Oats, *Chasmanthium latifolium* (USDA Zone 5), 3-5 feet tall.
This is a very valuable grass for the garden, as it is one of the few that will survive in summer shade. It is still listed as *Uniola latifolia* in most catalogs, where it's not too hard to find. The plant itself is very attractive, and the flowers make it unique. After the first frost, the leaves and flowers turn a rich tannish-brown and remain on the plant well into December. Sea Oats is a native of the eastern woods, and, on rare occasions, can still be found in the wild. The flowers are wonderful for dried arrangements.

Pampas Grass, *Cortaderia selloana* (USDA Zone 7), up to 14 feet.
This is the giant of the Ornamental Grasses found growing in the United States. The flowering plumes are really fantastic and have often been used in the movies to decorate everything from Cleopatra's barge to a Jean Harlow hotel suite. Although they are limited to Zone 7, and south, the northerner can still enjoy this stately plant by digging it up in the fall and storing it in the basement, never letting the plant dry out completely. Outside it needs full sun and fertile soil. Anticipate your future landscape if you plan to use Pampas Grass in a permanent position. This is the type of plant that can easily dominate almost any setting.

Always buy female plants, as the flowers are much more showy. The male flowers lack the covering of silky hairs. In addition to the white variety, Thompson & Morgan offers seed of other named forms of Pampas Grass that have colors of pinks, silvery whites, and yellows.

Bulbous Oat Grass
Arrhenatherum elatius var.
bulbosum 'Variegatum'

Reed Grass

Calamagrostis epigens

6
5
4
3
2
1
0

Northern Sea Oats

Chasmanthium latifolium

5

4

3

2

1

0

Pampas Grass
Cortaderia selloana

Lemon Grass, *Cymbopogon citratus* (USDA Zone 10), up to 6 feet.
Southern Florida, California, and Hawaii are the only states where it is warm enough to grow this plant out-of-doors. But don't despair, as it does very well in a pot under average home conditions. It will rarely exceed two feet in the house but will top six in the tropics. The flower, when it blooms, is non-descript, but the plant is very attractive with its arching leaves of light green. It makes a great conversation piece, for Lemon Grass is the commercial source of lemon oil, and a crushed leaf has a most wonderful smell and will always surprise everyone. When the roots come through the drainage hole, pot on to one size larger. Soil should be light with sand for good drainage. Fertilize monthly whenever growth is evident.

Cymbopogon Nardus is another aromatic member of this grass family and is the source of citronella.

Another grass that is extensively used for perfume oils is *Vetiveria zizanioides*, or as it is commonly called, Khus Khus. It's a very attractive grass that is planted for soil conservation on land terraces in the West Indies, and the roots are often woven into mats for floors. I'm still trying to get someone to bring back a plant to the cold Northeast, but without success.

Striped Orchard Grass, *Dactylis glomerata* 'Variegata' (USDA Zone 5), 1-2 feet tall.
Orchard Grass is a European import that now covers most of the United States and has some importance as a forage grass for cattle. Striped Orchard Grass is the variegated form and one of the most beautiful. It's green is the green of limes and should be an enchanting addition to any garden. The flowers are nice for a wild bouquet but nothing to write home about. This grass does well in sun or partial shade. I sent to England for it, and I have never regretted the effort. If you do succumb to its charms, plant it next to some Light Blue Flax (*Linum* spp.), for the combination is delightful.

Tufted Hairgrass, *Deschampsia caespitosa* (USDA Zone 4), 1-2 feet tall.
Tufted Hairgrass looks exactly like its name and, in addition, bears open panicles of delicate spikelets in late spring. This is another grass that will grow in partial to full shade. After sending away for a plant, I found it growing on the edge of a wood at a nearby field. It will also do fairly well in damp soil.

Weeping Love Grass, *Eragrostis curvula* (USDA Zone 5), 3-4 feet tall.
This type of Love Grass was originally native to the mountainous regions of Tanganyika and was introduced to America as an ornamental in 1927. It was again introduced in 1934, this time as a forage crop for abandoned or eroded land in the southern states. This is a very attractive grass that does best in full sun and fertile soil.

Purple Love Grass, *Eragrostis spectabilis* (USDA Zone 5), 18-24 inches tall.
In addition to a pleasing open form, Purple Love Grass has spikelets of a lovely shade of reddish-purple that seem to be a deeper shade where exposed to full sun. It is a happy inhabitant of sandy soil and is often found along either fresh or saltwater beaches. The axils of the branches of the panicles bear little tufts of white hair. This is a beautiful grass and a good subject for indoor arrangements, as it keeps very well.

Plume Grass, *Erianthus ravennae* (USDA Zone 5), up to 14 feet tall.
Plume Grass is another European import. It is a lovely fountain effect in light green that turns golden-brown after the frosts of autumn. In addition, it bears tall silvery-beige plumes at the end of summer. This grass requires full sun and a fertile garden soil. A bit of thought should go into its placement since Plume Grass does have a tendency to dominate almost any setting. It can be interrupted in flowering by an early frost, and I always protect it with large sheets of plastic the first few cold nights.

Lemon Grass
Cymbopogon citratus

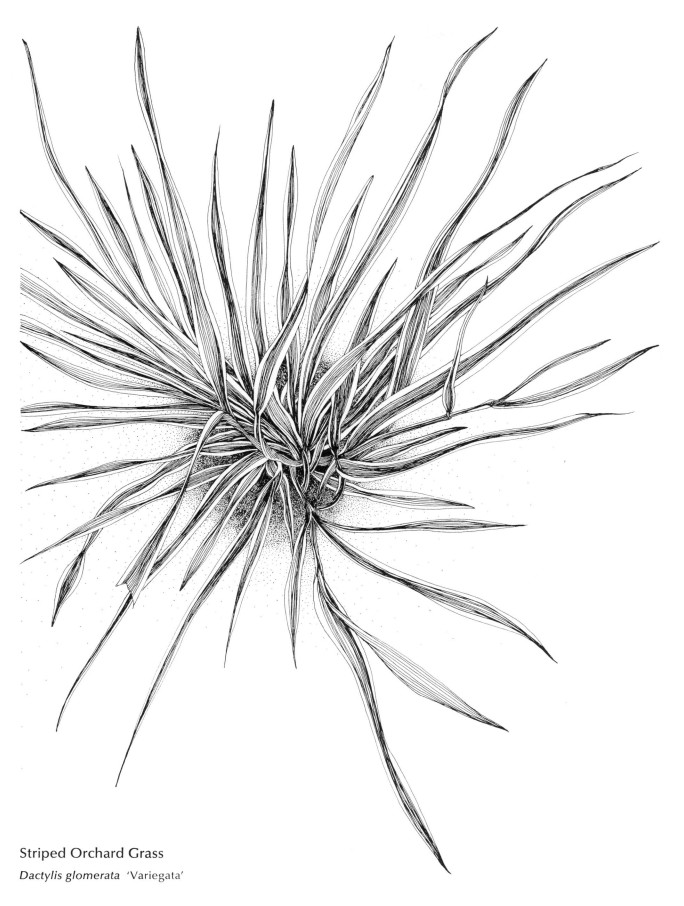

Striped Orchard Grass

Dactylis glomerata 'Variegata'

Tufted Hairgrass
Deschampsia caespitosa

Weeping Love Grass
Eragrostis curvula

Purple Love Grass
Eragrostis spectabilis

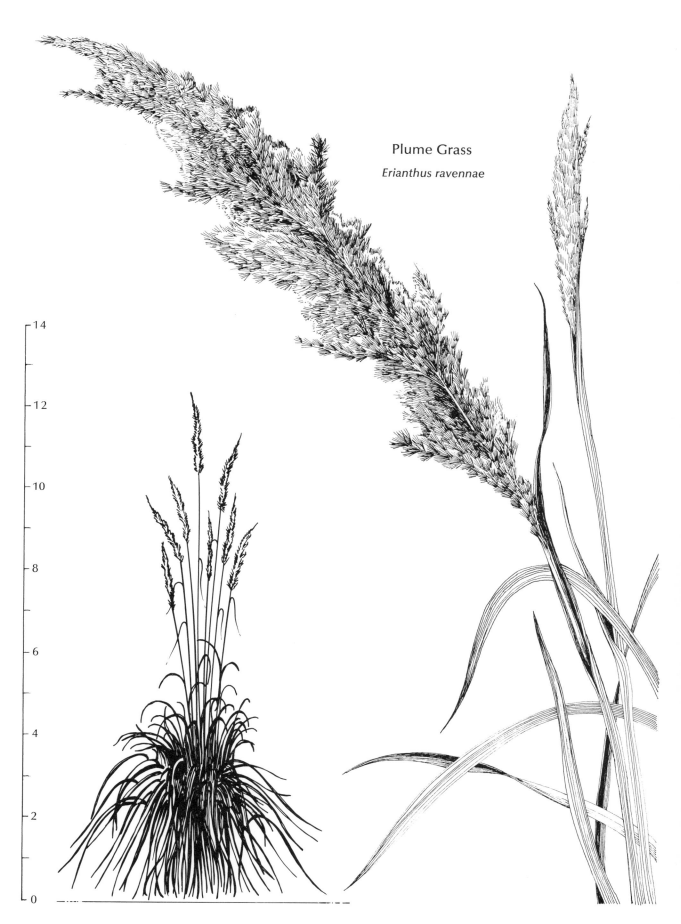

Plume Grass

Erianthus ravennae

14
12
10
8
6
4
2
0

Blue Fescue, *Festuca ovina* var. *glauca* (USDA Zone 4), 6-12 inches tall.
Blue Fescue is a variety of Sheeps' Fescue Grass. It has a bluish bloom, which is actually a powder that covers the leaf-blade surfaces and that will easily rub off. This bloom gives the plant a most beautiful appearance in any setting. These grasses are named for sheep (*ovina*), because those animals are reported to be miserable in a field without it. The name is derived from the Celtic word *fest*, meaning pasture. The plants require full sun and demand a well-drained soil. My soil is very heavy in clay, and in order to make my Blue Fescue flourish, I had to cut the soil heavily with sand and gravel to insure proper drainage. When planted in clusters, Fescues are a perfect foil for a rock garden.

Uva Grass, *Gynerium sagittatum*, to 40 feet tall.
This large and unusual grass is found only in central and tropical America and Florida, or occasionally in green-house cultivation. The leaves are six feet or more in length and about two and one-half inches wide. The densely flowered panicles arise from smooth, straight stems that the American Indians used for arrow shafts. I mention it here since it is often found for sale as a dried flower in many parts of the country, and for years I wondered what it was.

Hakonechlora macra 'Aureola' (USDA Zone 5), 12-24 inches tall.
There is, unfortunately, no common name for *Hakonechlora* in English, although I'm sure the Japanese have more than one for a plant as charming as this. It is a grass that closely resembles a bamboo, and there still seems to be some doubt about which it is. When my specimen flowered last fall, I learned too late to distinguish grasses from bamboos by flower structure and will have to try again this year to settle the dispute.

> The *R. H. S. Dictionary of Gardening* lists the following three cultivars:
> *Hakonechlora macra,* 'Aureola,' a warm yellow with green stripes
> *H. macra,* 'Albo-Aurea,' a white and golden-yellow variegation
> *H. macra,* 'Albo-Variegata,' a green and white variegation

Mr. George Schenck of the Wild Garden has recently informed me that he is now growing the original species, and I look forward to seeing it. Whatever type you choose, try this grass in a pot or a groundcover.

Russian Buffalo Grass, *Hierochloe australis* (USDA Zone 3), 12-18 inches tall.
There is no illustration for Russian Buffalo Grass; by the time I realized I had neglected to draw it, two feet of snow had fallen on the garden. It's another species of our American Sweet Grass or Holy Grass (*Hierochloe odorata*) often used by American Indians for a flavoring and for a weaving material for baskets and mats. Both species contain a chemical called coumarin, which imparts a sweet aromatic principle to the plants (it's also found in Sweet Clover). The Russian variety is described in *Flora of the U.S.S.R.* as a favorite food of bison in the Belovezha Thicket; hence the common name.

Neither of these grasses is particularly suited for the garden, so why grow them? The Russian grass is used to turn vodka to Zubrowka by merely adding three or four blades of grass to a quart of spirit. In a short time the sweet odor is imparted to the liquor. I haven't tried the American Grass but would assume the action is about the same. In addition, the smell of the grass is so lovely that it's worth keeping about for that reason alone.

Squirrel's-tail Grass, *Hordeum jubatum* (USDA Zone 5), 18-24 inches tall.
As a garden plant, Squirrel's-tail is a bit nondescript, and its only value is in the flowers that appear in late spring and early summer. Often seen along roadsides in the Northeast, the green and silky plumes are most beautiful as cut flowers. With great care they can be dried for further use, but they do shatter easily. This grass likes full sun and is quite at home in soils that others would strongly dislike. It grows readily from seed and has what is often termed "weedy character," inferring that it spreads easily and could take over.

Blue Fescue
Festuca ovina var. *glauca*

Uva Grass
Gynerium sagittatum

8
7
6
5
4
3
2
1
0

Hakonechlora macra 'Aureola'

Squirrel's-tail Grass

Hordeum jubatum

Bottlebrush Grass, *Hystrix patula* (USDA Zone 5), 3-4 feet tall.
Bottlebrush is a most attractive grass of the northeastern woodlands and received its name for obvious reasons. One of the few grasses to be at home in a shady position and damp soil, it's an excellent choice for a woodland garden or wildflower bed. The awned spikelets look well in dried arrangements. Another variety often found is *H. patula* var. *bigeloviana*, and in this case the lemmas are covered with short hairs. This species is very easily confused with the Wild Ryes and is a close relative.

Satintail Grass, *Imperata brevifolia* (USDA Zone 8), 3-4 feet tall.
Satintail grows in the deserts of the southwest United States and is rarely found in cultivation, as it can present problems as a weed. Still, it is often found in commercial shops as a dried flower, and since the normally silvery-haired panicles are easily dyed any number of ghastly colors, you have a good chance of finding it. When natural this grass is lovely; when dyed it is obnoxious.

Eulalia Grass, *Miscanthus sacchariflorus* (USDA Zone 5), 8-12 feet tall.
Miscanthus is a genus of ornamental grasses represented by two species and many varieties extensively cultivated in gardens throughout the world. Eulalia Grass *(M. sacchariflorus)* grows very tall and produces magnificent plumes of silvery spikelets that, unlike *M. sinensis,* are without awns. This is another grass that requires care in placement, as it can easily overwhelm the landscape. As the summer progresses, the bottom leaves die back, and by tearing them off you reveal more of the handsome stems. These stems become very dark and hard with age and exposure. After the growing season is over, the stems can be removed and will take a beautiful polish. In ancient Japan they were used to form many implements, such as brush handles and kitchen utensils. When your growing season is too short (less than ninety days), there can be some troubles with flowering. Try growing the plant in a 10- to 12-inch pot or tub so you can take it indoors when a frost is predicted. Make sure plenty of water and fertilizer are provided. Full sun is required for maximum development.

A dwarf form of Eulalia called *Miscanthus sacchariflorus* 'Dwarf', was imported from Japan by The Wild Garden and makes a truly great pot plant. The slender stems turn dark purple and trail over the edge of a pot.

A larger version of Eulalia called (as if you couldn't guess) Giant Eulalia (*M. sacchariflorus* 'Giganteus') is sometimes grown in the southernmost states and can easily top sixteen feet in one season.

Care should be taken with these grasses when grown in warm climates, since they spread by rhizomes and can take over large areas before you know it.

Eulalia Grass, *Miscanthus sinensis* (USDA Zone 5), 8-12 feet tall.
This form of Eulalia has panicles of pinkish-white flowers. Each spikelet has an awn that is lacking in *M. sacchariflorus*. *M. sinensis* forms large clumps in the landscape, not spreading by rhizomes. The other varieties of Eulalia whose descriptions follow are also clump-forming grasses.

Maiden Grass, *Miscanthus sinensis* 'Gracillimus' (USDA Zone 5), 6-8 feet tall.
This variant is properly named—both its common and scientific names—since the total form of the plant gives it the stance of a graceful maiden. The leaves are long, narrow, and lightly curved at the tips. The leaf color is light green, and the mid-rib is white. As with others of the *Miscanthus* species, full sun and fertile soil are needed.

Looking out of my studio window, the whole front garden is deep under snow, yet the light-brown leaves of this plant (and the other *Miscanthus*) are still visible against the winter landscape.

Bottlebrush Grass

Hystrix patula

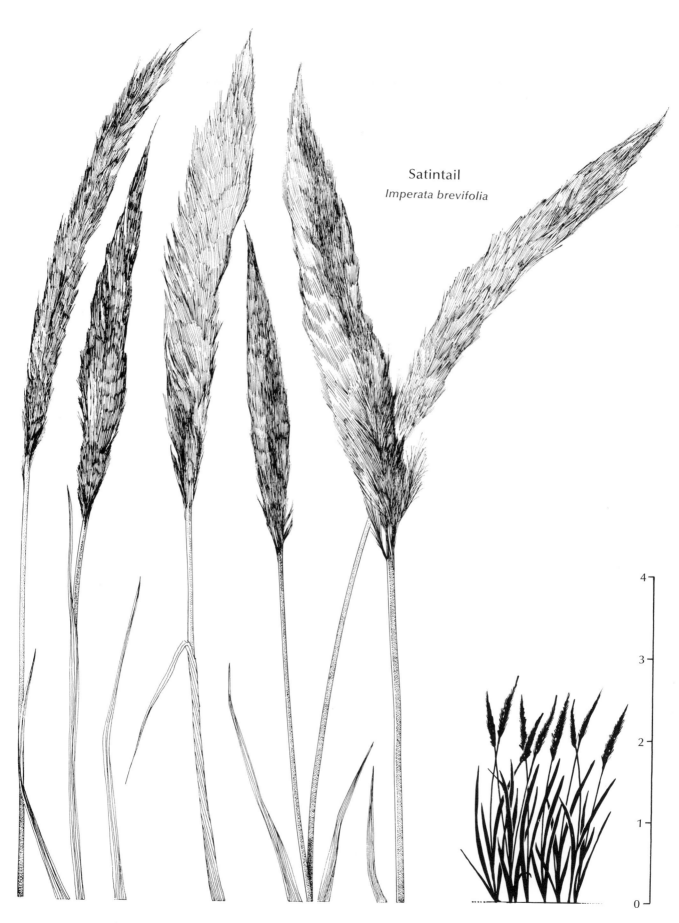

Satintail

Imperata brevifolia

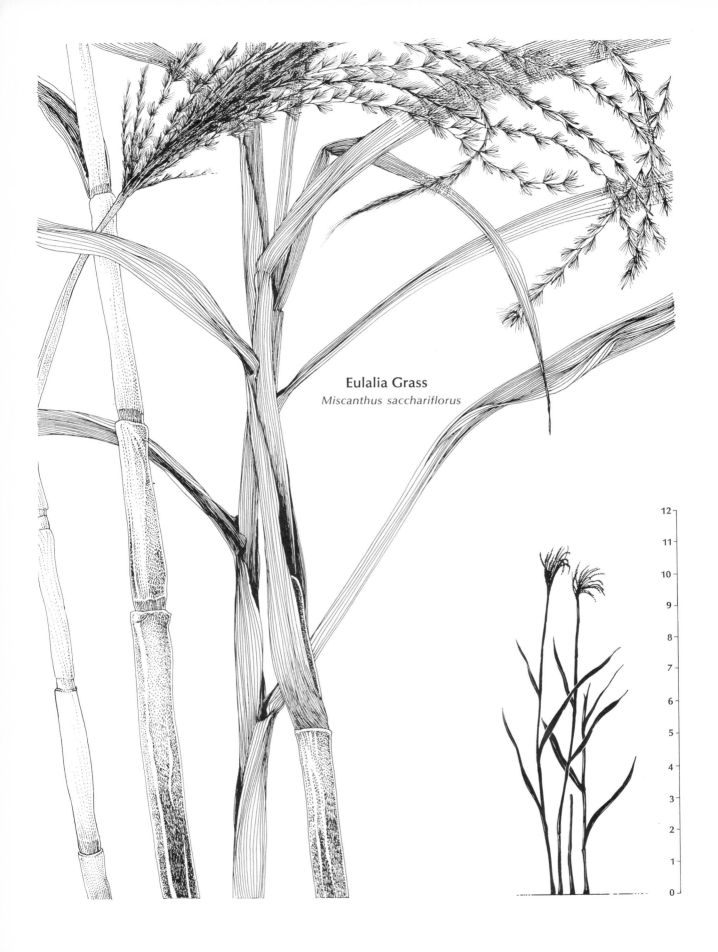

Eulalia Grass
Miscanthus sacchariflorus

12
11
10
9
8
7
6
5
4
3
2
1
0

Maiden Grass
Miscanthus sinensis
'Gracillimus'

Striped Eulalia
Grass
M. sinensis
'Variegatus'

Striped Eulalia Grass, *Miscanthus sinensis* 'Variegatus'
(USDA Zone 6), 4-6 feet tall.
This variegated form of *Miscanthus* requires some protection where temperatures below 0°F persist for any length of time. The overall effect of the leaves is very pleasant, and it is not too tall to cope with. Mine has never flowered but from botanical descriptions it closely matches the other plants in this genus.

Zebra Grass, *Miscanthus sinensis* 'Zebrinus' (USDA Zone 5), 6-8 feet tall.
Another close favorite of mine is Zebra Grass; it's a delight to any gardener who suffers through a northern winter. One is hard put to believe that any grass with such a tropical look could succeed where temperatures ever fall below freezing, even for an instant. The individual leaves are not striped but dashed with horizontal bands of a light golden-brown. Massive clumps are formed over the years with a true fountainlike effect. Flowers, as in other *Miscanthus* varieties, are large and showy, giving an added plus to a truly beautiful plant. While full sun is required for maximum growth, Zebra Grass will persist in damp soil, making it an excellent poolside choice. If any leaves sprout without the colored bands, be sure to cut them off so only the variegated forms have a chance to grow.

Purple Moor Grass, *Molinea caerulea* 'Variegata'
(USDA Zone 5), 18-24 inches.
This is another plant that originally came from Europe and has naturalized in the eastern United States. The variegated foliage forms a neat, compact mound that is useful in the flower garden or rock garden. It will accept partial shade and some dampness. It is said to succeed as a potted plant, but I've yet to try this. The flower spikes are too small to be of much use in a winter bouquet, but on the plant they are always a source of interest: as the panicles unfold, they, too, are variegated and give the impression that the spikelets have been banded with a brush of light yellow paint.

Basket Grass, *Oplismenus hirtellus* 'Variegatus'
This is one of the few grasses widely used as a potted plant. It originally comes from Africa and is easily confused with the *Tradescantias* of houseplant fame. Basket Grass is perfect as a hanging plant, and the white and purple striped leaves sparkle as long as they're allowed plenty of sun and water. During active growth, feed them bi-monthly with any houseplant fertilizer. The stems root at the nodes, so to propagate, simply push a node into the dirt and hold down with a small stone or bobby-pin. They have a tendency to fall prey to spider mite. If you have trouble with this, try washing the leaves every few days for a week or two with soapy water. If you forget to water and the plant dries, or if the mites are too much, sheer the stems back to the surface of the dirt, and it will sprout anew.

Switch Grass, *Panicum virgatum* (USDA Zone 4), 4-6 feet tall.
Switch Grass is one of the most valuable native grasses of the prairies. While not entirely suited for the more formal perennial garden, it's a natural for a mass planting in a local field or when used as a screen to block out an unwanted subject, it gives an excellent effect. The open panicles are very attractive when viewed against a dark background. Switch Grass will withstand poor drainage and flooding, growing with wet feet for weeks without visible discomfort. Of the three most valuable Prairie Grasses—Big Bluestem, Switch Grass, and Indiangrass—Switch Grass is the first to mature. A summer of native American grasses and a natural succession of seedings can be had by using these three grasses in a group planting.

Zebra Grass

Miscanthus sinesis
'Zebrinus'

Miscanthus sacchariflorus 'Dwarf'

Purple Moor Grass

Molinea caerulea 'Variegata'

3

2

1

0

Basket Grass
Oplismenus hirtellus 'Variegatus'

Switch Grass
Panicum virgatum

Fountain Grass, *Pennisetum alopecuroides* (USDA Zone 5), 3-4 feet tall.
This particular Fountain Grass is one of the more popular ornamental grasses. I have no drawing, since my specimen was one of many plants ingested by our local herd of deer. It has a form that looks well in the back of a perennial border or in groups surrounded by a cut lawn. The flowers generally resemble those of *Pennisetum setaceum* but are more brown than red.

Crimson Fountain Grass, *Pennisetum setaceum* (USDA Zone 7), 2-3 feet tall.
Crimson Fountain Grass (once called *Pennisetum ruppellii*) is a lovely grass with attractive flowers and a graceful, fountain form. It is doubtful that this grass is hardy where temperatures fall below 0°F for any length of time, but I suggest that the gardener lift the plants in the fall, as with the *Miscanthus* species, since a grass as fine as this should not be lost. It will bloom from seed in the first year, but if you live with a short growing season (ninety days or less), start the seeds indoors in individual peat pots. The flowers can be used in dried arrangements only if picked well before final opening and then handled with the utmost care.

Gardener's Garters, *Phalaris arundinacea* picta (USDA Zone 4), 3-4 feet tall.
Phalaris has been grown as an ornamental for so many years that it has acquired a number of common names, among them: Ribbon Grass, Whistle Grass (when a blade is held between the fingers and given a hearty blow, it emits a piercing whistle), Painted Grass, Gardener's Gators, and the above mentioned Garters. If one grass is to be found in old and forgotten country gardens, this is it.

Phalaris will grow in just about any soil, but if planted in full sun and fertile ground, it will spread in all directions; in very poor ground this is not a problem. In order to maintain a sizable group of these grasses, surround the initial planting with metal stripping to contain the roots. The flowers are attractive on the plants but are not fine enough for bouquets. The leaves start to brown at midsummer.

This grass is unusual because it will survive when the roots are submerged in water, so it become a valuable addition to the water garden. Just plant specimens in clay pots with a good, fertile soil, covering the soil surface with a layer of pea gravel to keep it from muddying the water, and gently submerge the pot, leaving three inches between the gravel and water surface.

Reed Grass, *Phragmites australis* (USDA Zone 4), up to 15 feet.
Fossil evidence of this grass has been found in Europe, making it literally one of the oldest grasses known. It grows on all the continents of the world and has different uses for various cultures. In England, for example, it has been used to thatch roofs and to make fences and even some types of furniture. In our American west, the Indians used this most adaptable plant to make lattices for adobe huts, rugs and mats, shafts for arrows, and even portable nets. While too large and demanding for the ordinary garden, it makes a visual statement all the year round. If you have a damp and poorly drained site that will support little else, Reed Grass will do very well. Along the highway ditches of the country, this grass continues to provide the only interest available for miles, since many other types of vegetation have been destroyed by highway departments.

The panicle pictured was picked before the spikelets began to open, and now in midwinter, it still has the deep purple-brown color that fades as the flowers develop. *Phragmites* is Latin for reed.

I've never seen it offered for sale, but quick work with a shovel should keep any gardener in good supply, as this grass spreads quickly.

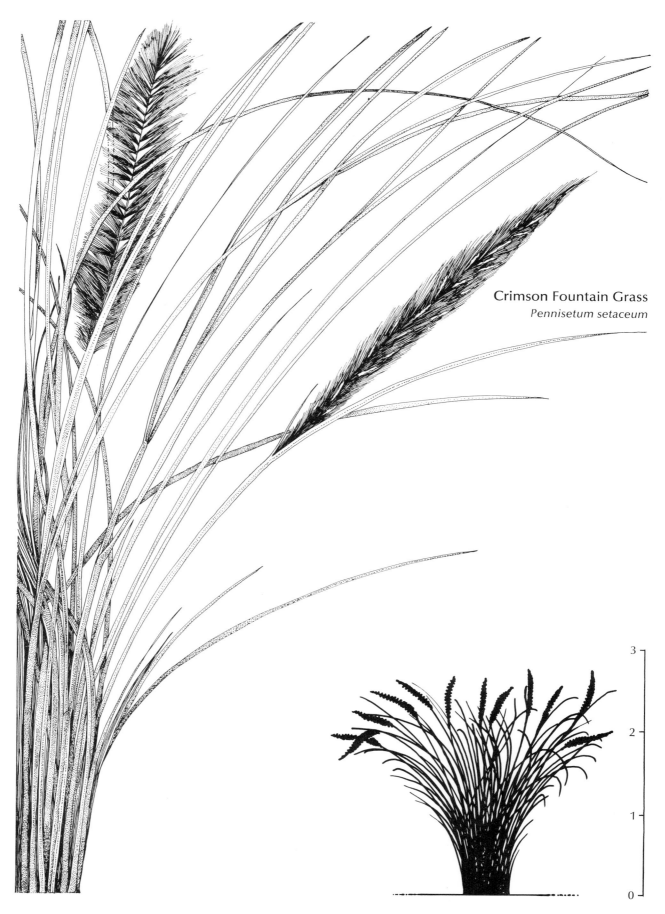

Crimson Fountain Grass
Pennisetum setaceum

3

2

1

0

Gardener's Garters

Phalaris arundinacea
 var. picta

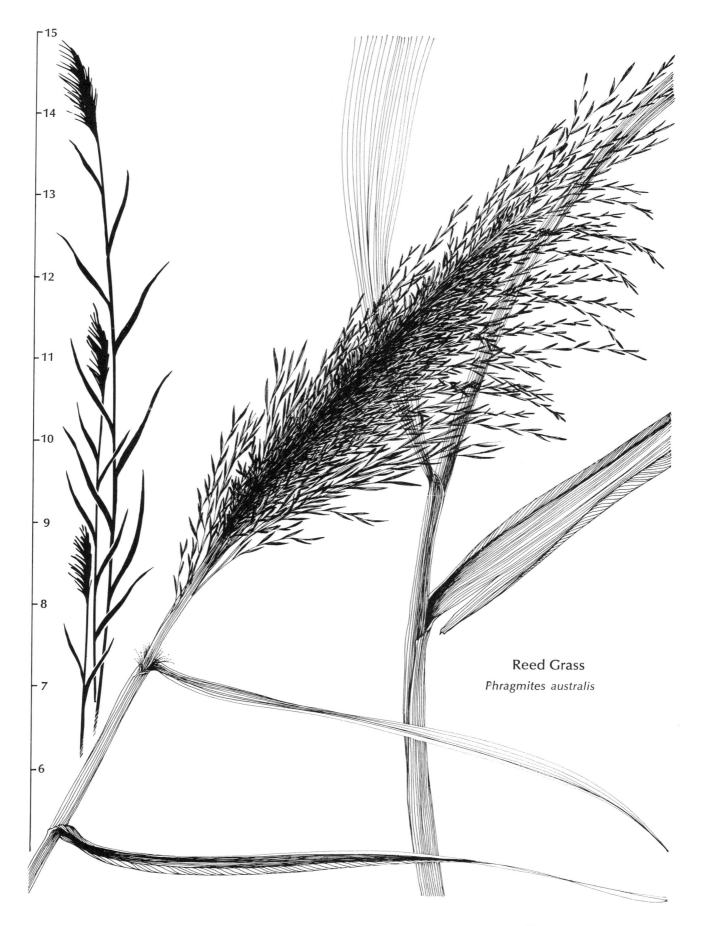

Reed Grass
Phragmites australis

Indian Grass, *Sorghastrum avenaceum* (USDA Zone 5), 4-5 feet tall.
This is the last of the Big Three Prairie Grasses. It does well in almost any condition and matures to bear flowers and seeds late in the season. Named for the American Indian, the spikelets bear bright yellow anthers which turn golden-brown after the autumn frost, when the foliage turns bright orange. While the panicles are not overly showy in winter bouquets, the color is a welcome addition.

Cord Grass, *Spartina pectinata* (USDA Zone 5), up to 8 feet tall.
Often when a certain plant becomes an integral part of a culture, it is known by many common names. Cord Grass has many, including: Bull-Grass, Tall Marsh-Grass, Slough Grass (*slough* is an old Anglo-Saxon word meaning a wet or marshy place), Freshwater Cord Grass, and my favorite, Upland-Creek Stuff. Once a dominant grass of the tall grass prairies of the northcentral United States, Cord Grass does well on wet or damp soil, often aiding in soil conservation. The pioneers of America used this grass to thatch roofs and protect haystacks against the weather. It is used today in the construction of archery targets.

Too tall for most gardens, this grass makes an excellent backdrop and is well-suited for water or poolside planting. The plant turns yellow after the frosts, and the one-sided panicles are an attractive addition to the dried bouquet.

If you're lucky enough to have a seaside garden, try this grass to aid in binding sand against the winds.

St. Augustine Grass, *Stenotaphrum secundatum* 'Variegatum'
(USDA Zone 7), 4-12 inches tall.
St. Augustine Grass spreads quickly by stolons and with great dispatch. It's often used as a lawn grass in the South, where it responds quite well to mowing. The cultivar pictured has leaves striped with white and makes an excellent potted plant in the North. But make sure that, like for all grasses, there is plenty of light. Since the stems (or stolons) root easily at the nodes, I take cuttings from the mother plant in early spring and use the resultant plants as an interesting bedding material outdoors during summer. As long as the soil is well-drained and the grass gets full sun, it does beautifully until late fall.

Feather Grass, *Stipa pennata* (USDA Zone 5), 2-3 feet tall.
There are over one hundred species of perennial grasses belonging to the genus *Stipa*. Their narrow leaves and long single-flowered spikelets gracefully dot many plains and savannas of the world.

Feather Grass bears conspicuously bearded awns, one to each potential seed. It needs an open, sunny position in fertile, well-drained soil. It does double duty as a lovely garden plant and necessary part of many good dried arrangements. If grown from seed, the plant will not flower until the second year, so try to get mature plants.

Stipa calamagrostis is a taller species that bears violet awns and forms dense thickets.

A wild *Stipa* of the northcentral prairies of the United States, Porcupine Grass (*Stipa spartea*) uses the unique twisted awn of this genus to guarantee its future seed germination. When the floret falls from the flower stem, it sticks the pointed end into the earth where barbed hairs prevent it from pulling out. The awn then coils and uncoils with changes in humidity, and when it luckily lodges itself under a stem or other ground debris that provides support, the seed proceeds to drill itself into the earth. This procedure poses quite a problem to livestock that come upon the seeds. Occasionally *Stipa spartea* is available from nurseries as a plant, and it makes a unique addition to a naturalized garden.

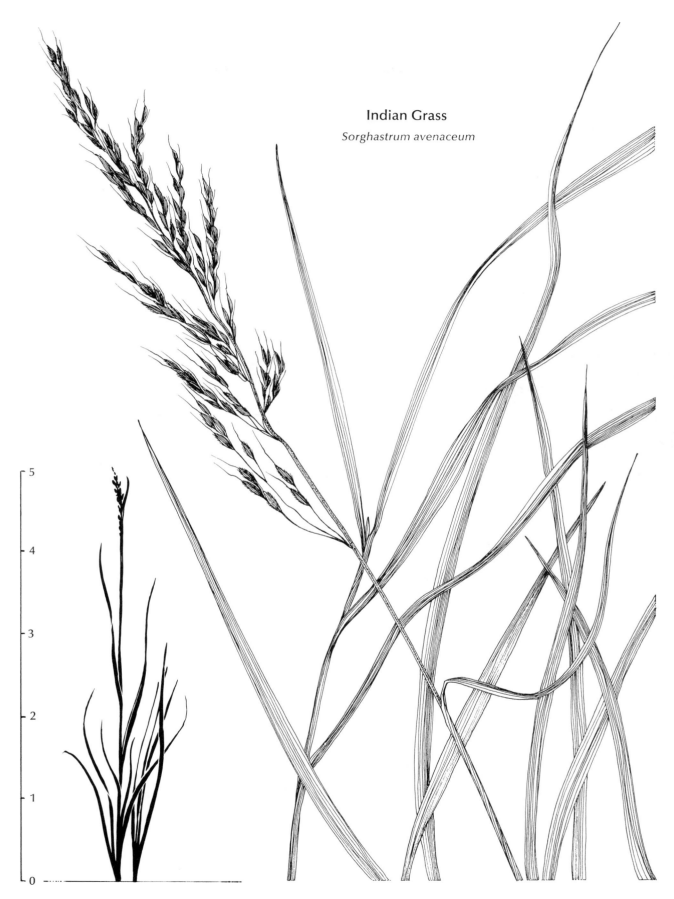

Indian Grass

Sorghastrum avenaceum

5

4

3

2

1

0

Cord Grass
Spartina pectinata

7

6

5

4

3

2

1

0

St. Augustine Grass
Stenotaphrum secundatum
'Variegatum'

Feather Grass
Stipa pennata

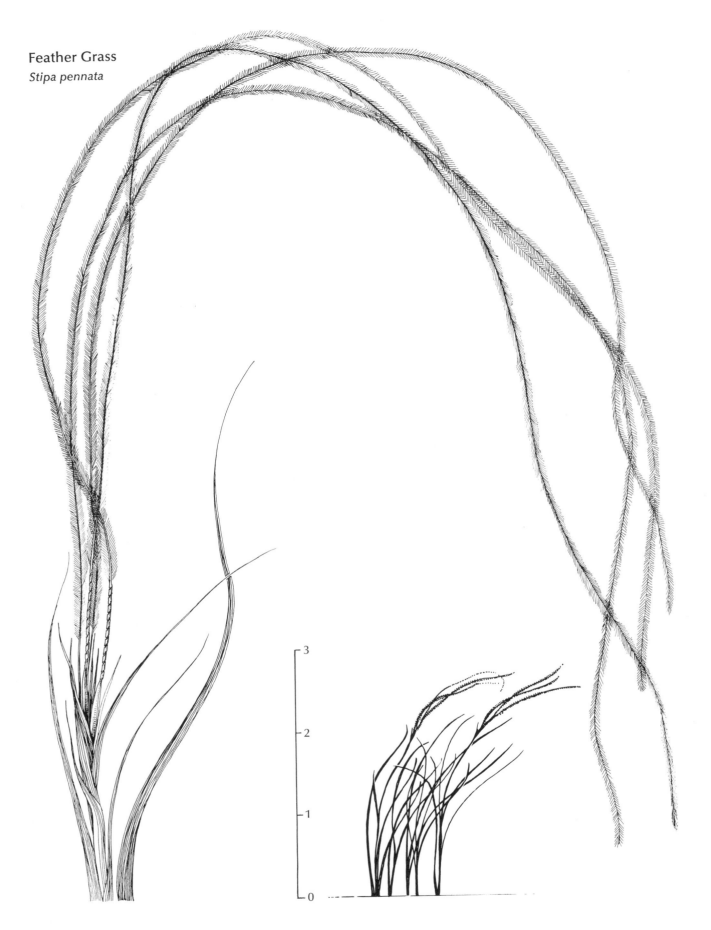

There are many more perennial grasses worthy of consideration. In a future revision, I hope to add some of the following:

Giant Reed Grass, *Arundo donax*, a truly unique grass that is used to manufacture clarinet and saxophone reeds;

Mosquito Grass, *Bouteloua gracilis*, with its one-sided panicles that resemble miniature brown combs;

Blue Lyme Grass, *Elymus arenarius*, with its lovely light blue foliage;

Sand Love Grass, *Eragrostis trichodes*, known for its gentle weeping form;

Reed Meadow Grass, *Glyceria aquatica variegata*, a beautiful rushlike grass for waterside planting;

Variegated Velvet Grass, *Holcus lanatus albo-variegatus*, a charming variegated form of a pasture grass and weed;

Melica ciliata, an excellent candidate for rock-gardens.

Koeleria gracilis with its creamy-white panicles and tufted leaves;

Bulbous Bluegrass, *Poa bulbosa*, a grass that replaces the seeds of the flower with tiny bulbs;

and, I trust, many, many more.

Gray's Sedge
Carex Grayi

Great Pendulous Wood Sedge
Carex pendula

4

3

2

1

0

The Sedges and Rushes

"WHERE IS THIS STRANGER? RUSHES, LADIES, RUSHES,
RUSHES AS GREEN AS SUMMER FOR THIS STRANGER."
— Beaumont and Fletcher, *Valentinian*

THE SEDGES

Sedges are grasslike perennial herbs that belong to the family Cyperaceae. The true sedges are found in the genus *Carex*, of which there are well over 500 species. These plants are easily identified from grasses by their three-ranked leaves, often rolled and threadlike, and their triangular stems that are solid rather than hollow and all having a pithy center. While the sedges lack large and brightly colored flowers, they still possess stamens and pistils, and produce tiny, leathery nuts as seeds. Much of their interest to the gardener lies in their fresh green color and the fantastic shapes of many of the fruiting bodies.

On a scale of 1 to 10 in economic value, most people would probably give them a generous − 50, but the sedges are valuable members of the plant world. While a few grow on dry ground, most are plants of cool and temperate regions and revel in swamps, pool borders, ditches, river banks, and marshes. Here they form an intermediate step between useless mud (to man) and valuable dry land by spreading their rhizomes and acting as a landfill that eventually allows other vegetation to grow.

Since the stems are very dry and lack most starches and sugars, sedges are of little use as animal food, although the Sea Club Rush (*Scirpus maritimus*), a common species found growing in salt marshes on most seacoasts of the world (and not a true rush), has sweet rootstocks and is used in Sweden for pig food. The Common Bulrush (*Scirpus lacustris*) is often utilized in the manufacture of rush-bottomed chairs (and this plant is not a true Rush, either). The Earth Almond or Zulu Nut (*Cyperus esculentus* var. *sativus*) produces an edible tuber that is roasted for food and ground for flour (although there is an argument raging between its use as a food and its potential threat as a noxious weed).

Leatherleaf Sedge, *Carex Buchananii* (USDA Zone 5), 12-18 inches tall.
As with many sedges, the leaves on this plant are round and taper to a curled point; this delicate form is matched with an attractive red-brown color, making this is a valuable garden addition. Leatherleaf is named for the texture of the leaf, which is tough. The plant likes a moist location and prefers to be shaded from the noon sun. When temperatures fall below 10°F, this sedge needs either snow cover or a winter mulch for protection. Leatherleaf is not always easy to find in the United States and originally came from New Zealand.

Bowles' Golden Sedge, *Carex stricta* 'Bowles' Golden'
(USDA Zone 4), 1-2 feet tall.
This is a lovely sedge named after the great English gardener, Edward A. Bowles, who was an innovative force in the landscape at the beginning of this century. Bowles' Golden is a cultivar of a species common to the northern

United States and usually found in swamps. Its color is a rich golden-yellow, and the sedge should be planted in shallow water, so that its "feet" are always wet. Another plant that you will most likely import.

Gray's Sedge, *Carex Grayi* (USDA Zone 4), 1-2 feet tall.
This sedge makes a handsome clump of light green leaves with a papery texture that are alive well into the fall. While adaptable to most soils and locations, it does prefer moist soil and good sun. It's happy by poolside. The flowers develop in mid- to late summer, and the resultant fruiting body looks for all the world like the glass and wrought-iron hanging lights found in hallways of Spanish stucco houses of the twenties. Gray's Sedge is often found growing in the wild, especially by streams and brooks in open woods.

Japanese Sedge Grass, *Carex Morrowii* var. *expallida*
(USDA Zone 5), 6-12 inches tall.
As Mr. Schneck of the Wild Garden has sagely observed, here is a simple plant that has become a "pop plant" and hit the big time. It always surprises me that with all the beautiful and useful sedges available, the only one offered by most big nurseries in the United States is this one. All this doesn't mean that it's not a good plant to have. The gracefully arched leaves are striped with creamish-white and green and persist well into winter, when it's a wistful reminder of summer, because the leaves cast shadows on the snow. Sedge Grass prefers a moist location with some shade from the hot mid-day sun.

As a pot plant, Japanese Sedge is excellent in a potting mixture of peat moss, potting soil, and sand—one-third each. Make sure it receives adequate light, and generally it will bloom. The flowers are not resplendent, as they resemble crushed camel's-hair brushes that have been dipped in yellow powder, but they are a welcome sight in late winter, the time when mine generally appear.

The Great Pendulous Wood Sedge, *Carex pendula* (USDA Zone 5), 2-4 feet tall.
This is a European relative of the sedges, and the name alone makes it worth a try in the garden. It's a relative, naturally, of the Lesser Pendulous Wood Sedge (*Carex sylvatica*) and the Lesser Marsh Sedge (*Carex acutiformis*) and is one of the tallest of these grasslike plants. A well-grown specimen becomes a fountain of light green leaves, with the spikelets on very thin stems forming graceful arches of brownish-green. When a light summer breeze rustles the leaves, it sounds like unwrapping the tissue paper in a Christmas present. If put in a final position and not moved, these plants will make a sizable statement. They need, like most sedges, moist soil and some shade from the hot sun.

Plantain-leaved Sedge, *Carex plantaginea* (USDA Zone 5), 12-18 inches tall.
This sedge is named after the common weed with the wide green leaves that inhabits lawns, and if anyone ever develops a variety of this weed with more attractive flowers, it will become a bestseller. The sedge is much more useful when the leaves reach a length of twelve inches and make quite a statement when planted in groups. It closely resembles Fraser's Sedge, but its flowers are not as showy.

Miniature Variegated Sedge, *Carex conica variegata*
(USDA Zone 7[?]), to 4 inches tall.
A truly beautiful little plant from Japan. I think it will be hardy outdoors with protection in Zone 5, but I'm not sure, and this plant does so well in a small clay pot that I might never know. The deep green and curved leaves are edged with white, and the white is applied with great precision. Good light and moist soil are the requirements. Lack of humidity and a too warm environment will cause the leaves to brown.

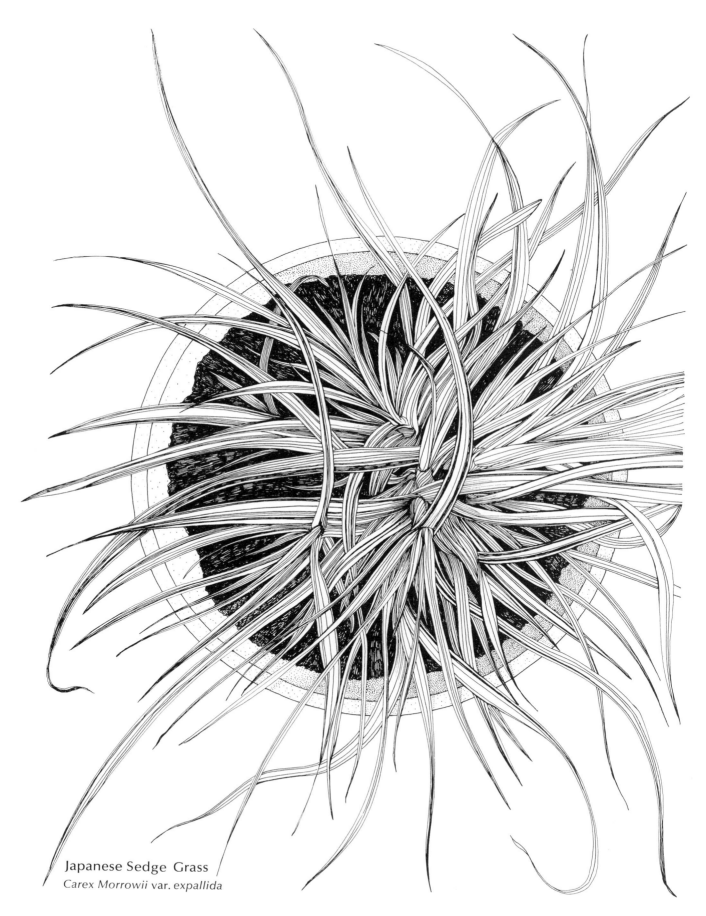

Japanese Sedge Grass
Carex Morrowii var. *expallida*

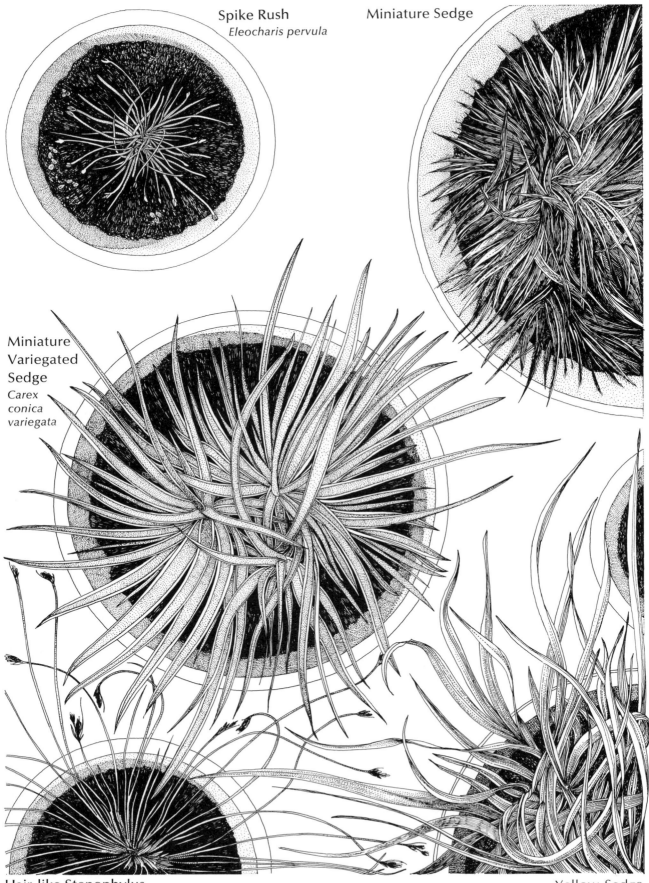

Spike Rush
Eleocharis pervula

Miniature Sedge

**Miniature
Variegated
Sedge**
*Carex
conica
variegata*

Hair-like Stenophylus
Stenophyllus capillaris

Yellow Sedge
Carex flava

Yellow Sedge, *Carex flava* (USDA Zone 5), to 12 inches tall.
Here is a plant common to both England and the United States, found in marshy areas and swampy pastures. The leaves are slender, a light yellow-green, and the plant does well in a pot. The flowers, like those of many sedges, are very unusual: the inch-long terminal spike is a yellow-brown, followed by three egg-shaped fruits made up of tiny shapes of green teardrops that are puffed up with air and have little recurved beaks. The flowers persist well into fall, and the plant naturalizes well, spreading by creeping rhizomes.

Carex foliosissima albo-mediana (USDA Zone 7 [?]), to 18 inches tall.
Another sedge originating in Japan and often grown as a houseplant in Europe but rarely seen in the United States. It's a tufted, grasslike form, but the leaves are tall and elegant with margins edged with a thin white stripe.

Hair-like Stenophylus, *Stenophyllus capillaris* (Annual), less than 10 inches tall.
This is an annual sedge first given to me by a rock-gardening friend, Budd Meyers of Hawley, Pa. The name in Latin means small, leaflike hairs, and it's a perfect description for this diminutive member of the Sedge Family. The tiny, threadlike structure works well not only in a rock garden, but in small pots, where the seed is easily gathered to start the plants anew for the following season. Stenophylus does well in any soil (even gravel), either wet or dry.

Spike Rush, *Eleocharis pervula* (USDA Zone 5), to one-inch tall.
Spike Rush—not a true rush—belongs to a relatively small genus of sedges that either grow under water, like Hair Grass (*Eleocharis acicularis*), or at the water's edge. The name in Greek is *helos*, a marsh, and *chairo*, I rejoice, which is a scholarly way of saying: I like it wet! If allowed to grow undisturbed in a happy position, Spike Rush will eventually form a lovely and tiny green carpet. It also excels as a pot subject if the soil is both well-drained and continually damp. Protect from noon-day summer sun. A hand-lens or microscope is a good adjunct to growing the Spike Rush. All parts of this plant need magnification to truly appreciate its tiny structure, especially the seeds; weelike compressed cylinders with cross-hatched lines or dots.

Fraser's Sedge, *Cymophyllus Fraseri* (USDA Zone 5), 12-18 inches tall.
Fraser's Sedge is the only member of the genus Cymophyllus and differs from *Carex* in not having more than one blade per stem. I was introduced to this plant by Bebe Miles, who has had extraordinary luck with this sedge in her beautiful wildflower gardens. Like all the others, it needs a good, moist soil and does its best along a stream or pool. The flowers are very showy and look more like a typical wildflower than a sedge. The evergreen leaves are large and straplike, and it blooms in early spring. Mrs. Miles has suggested that if it doesn't rain or the surrounding terrain is not damp enough, you've got to be prepared to water this plant to guarantee survival. Fraser's is definitely hardy to Pennsylvania, but it will succeed in Zone 5 if given winter protection with snow or a prepared mulch.

Egyptian Papyrus, *Cyperus Papyrus* (Tender Perennial), up to 8 feet (or taller).
Also called the Egyptian Paper Plant, this is the famous species of ancient reknown used in the manufacture of paper since 2750 B.C. It has also been used for thatching roofs, making rafts by tying the stems together in bundles, and distilling for alcohol. Put the plant in a clay pot of at least an eight-inch diameter and use a soil-mix of three parts of heavy top soil and one part of well-rotted or bagged cow manure. Stop the soil about an inch from the pot top and fill the rest with small, crushed stone or gravel to keep the dirt from muddying up the water. The water should cover the gravel by at least three inches. Give full sun. At summer's end, either discard the plant or bring indoors to a heated greenhouse; or try it as a houseplant, keeping its pot continually wet.

Fraser's Sedge

Cymophyllus Fraseri

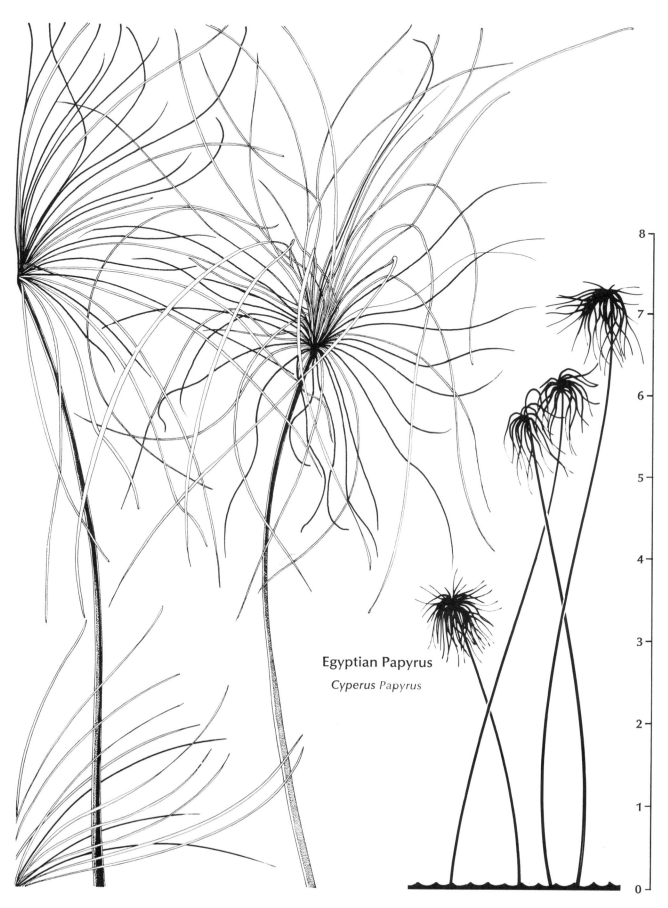

Egyptian Papyrus

Cyperus Papyrus

8

7

6

5

4

3

2

1

0

Umbrella Plant, *Cyperus alternifolius* (Tender Perennial), up to 3 feet tall.
This is a popular house plant for indoors and poolside (or even in the pool), having ribbed stems of a bright grassy green topped with a rosette of grasslike leaves much like the spokes of an umbrella. In the spring, brownish-green flowers grow above the crown of the leaves. After a summer outside, let it spend the winter with its pot in a saucer of water. In addition, these are other umbrella plants:

Dwarf Umbrella Plant (*Cyperus alternifolius gracilis*), a dwarf form growing only to about 12 inches tall.

Variegated Umbrella Plant (*Cyperus alternifolius variegatus*) is like the regular plant except that the leaves are handsomely striped with white. Any green leaves that appear should be removed to ensure that the variegations persist.

Broadleaf Umbrella Palm (*Cyperus diffusus*) is more squat and bushy than the others of this genus. The stem is very triangular, and the broad leaves have a rough edge that you can easily feel with your finger.

Striped Umbrella Palm (*Cyperus diffusus variegatus*) The leaves are striped with pale yellow and cream on green.

Cotton-Grass, *Eriophorum angustifolium* (USDA Zone 5), 1-2 feet tall.
In the tundras of the Arctic, vast areas are covered with the snowy-white "blooms" of Cotton-Grass. The Latin name is *erion*, wool, and *phero*, I bear. They are bog plants of easy cultivation and may be propagated by seeds and division. There are ten or more species that occur naturally in the United States, but *E. angustifolium* is the only type available commercially. Formerly, the stems and roots of these plants were thought to have medicinal value because of the astringent quality of the plant juice. The "cotton" comes from long and fine bristles that cover the spikelets. The soft down has been gathered for pillow stuffing, and a paper has been manufactured from pressing the silky hairs. Some attempts have been made at manufacturing cloth, but the fibers are too short to twist well. Altogether a unique and interesting plant for the poolside.

Miniature Bulrush, *Scirpus cernuus* (USDA Zone 8), up to 12 inches tall.
The bulrushes and their relatives are part of the genus *Scirpus*. They are denizens of the swamp, marsh, river-edge, and the vast salt-water tidal marshes that occur in the United States and Europe. They are increased by either seed or division. Used mostly in naturalized areas of a water garden, the Miniature Bulrush is also handsome as a house plant when grown in a sandy soil with the pot standing in a saucer of water. Its graceful, grasslike tufts grow up to a foot tall and often are tipped with tiny white flowers.

American Great Bulrush, *Scirpus validus* (USDA Zone 4), up to 9 feet tall.
The American Great Bulrush and its European relative, *Scirpus lacustris*, are among the most noble of the native water plants, and one specimen in a small pool is indeed a striking sight. Umbels of chocolate-brown flowers are borne near the stem tops, and the dark green, tough leaves are still used for caning chairs and making mats and ropes. It's also said to be employed in manufacturing a type of paper called "Teele" in California. Grow the bulrush in a six- to eight-inch pot using the same soil mix as with papyrus, topping with the layer of stone or gravel and putting in water with a level of three to five inches above the top of the pot. For the winter, the pot may be left frozen if it's buried in the earth with the plant root within. If left above ground exposed to the daily weather changes, the root will die.

Cotton-Grass

Eriophorum angustifolium

2 —

1 —

0

Wool-Grass

Scirpus cyperinus

6

5

4

3

2

1

0

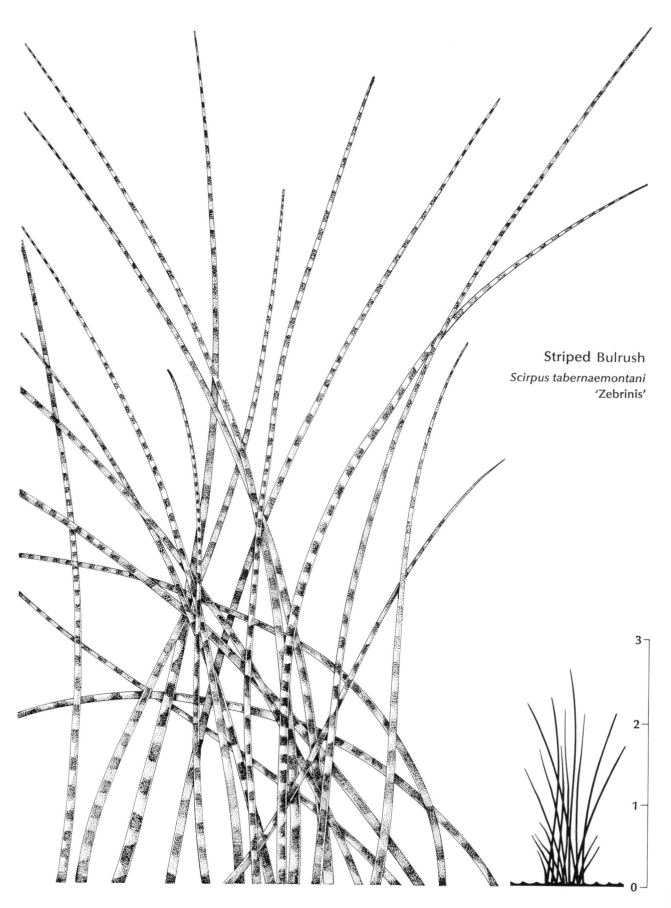

Striped Bulrush

Scirpus tabernaemontani
'Zebrinis'

3

2

1

0

Wood Bulrush or Clubrush, *Scirpus sylvaticus* (USDA Zone 4), 4-6 feet tall.
This bulrush is smaller than *validus*. Its stems are coarser, more grasslike, and a deeper green. The greenish-brown umbels of flowers often stretch eight inches across. Follow the same instructions as for *validus*.

Wool-Grass, *Scirpus cyperinus* (USDA Zone 4), up to 6 feet tall.
Most people would consider this plant too weedy for a formal garden, and I'd agree. However, in a naturalized area of poor and damp soil, Wool-Grass excels. Its graceful leaves wave in the wind, and the clusters of flowers add interest until late in the fall. This is an excellent plant for dried arrangements; the spikelets soon are covered with wool threads, looking for all the world like "pills" on a wool sweater.

Striped Bulrush, *Scirpus tabernaemontani* 'Zebrinis'
          (USDA Zone 6), 2-3 feet tall.
A most beautiful plant that will draw rave notices wherever it's found, Striped Bulrush should be found in every poolside or water garden. Sometimes called the Porcupine Plant, this gem originally hails from Japan. It grows best naturalized in shallow water but will do reasonably well in pots. If given adequate winter protection, I'm sure it would survive in Zone 5. Like many variegated plants, keep it out of full summer sun; a lightly shaded position is best.

THE RUSHES
Rushes belong to a rather small family of plants, the Juncaceae. The name derives from the Latin word, *juncere*, rush, and most likely refers to the uses of rushes in furniture manufacture.

Most of the rushes come from cold and barren lands. They differ from sedges in having six petals surrounding the flowers. Like the sedges, their main value to nature is in binding the soil.

They have had a few notable uses for man, and one has lasted throughout English history. Before the general use of carpets appeared on the economic horizon, rushes were gathered, mixed with herbs and flowers, and then strewn upon the floors, to help brighten things up. Naturally the country folk had the sources of local wetlands and swamps, but the cities, like London during Elizabethan days, had to import rushes; by the time that the carting charges were paid, these trifles for the floors of the well-off city-dweller could be expensive. One of the charges of extravagance leveled against Cardinal Wolsey, was "that he caused his floors to be strewn with rushes too frequently"; but since table manners of those days were not of the best, and animals were usually fed at the table, the floor rushes must have speedily become unwholesome, and the Cardinal can hardly be faulted for changing them whenever he could.

Soon, large rush-carts were constructed of rushes staked on wagons, with a hole at the top for a young man to sit beneath and thrust a living tree through the opening. The wagons were often covered with white cloths and decorated with borrowed treasures like silver tankards and cream jugs, then adorned with ribbons, and preceded by young men and women streaming with ribbons, dancing the Morris-dance, in celebration of the "Gathering of the Rushes." (The Morris-dance was a Spanish import and originally called the Moor Dance.)

This celebration was not held in spring, as one might expect, but in August, when the rushes were gathered for the coming winter to be used in local churches for covering the draughty floors against the cold. As a custom, the Rush Cart persisted well into the nineteenth century. Now, except for a few very isolated villages, it has gone the way of many pleasant and valuable memories of the past.

RUSH CART

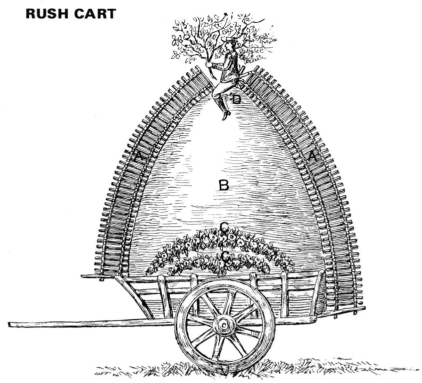

SIDE VIEW.

BACK VIEW

The part A is composed of bundles of the longest Rushes of about 2 inches diameter, neatly tied with twine.

B. The Rushes cut and shewing white, being laid across.

C Projects over the wheels and cut, the edges being adorned with carnations &c.

D A man and some oak branches

E Ends of the bolts or bundles cut straight shewing the white ends

G Extreme breadth.

From *Rush-Bearing,* by Alfred Burton (Manchester: Brook and Chrystal, 1891).

Common Rush, *Juncus effusus* (USDA Zone 4), up to 3 feet.
A common plant in wet and swampy conditions across the world, the rush will also be found occasionally in very poor and dry soil. The root-stock is of the creeping variety, and the stems are pale-green, very pliant, and end in a point. There are no leaves, except for a few brown wrappings at the base of the plants. The flowers occur half-way up the stems, forming side-panicles of greenish-brown spikelets. When plants are used in groups with a naturalized area, the dense clumps are most attractive and persist well into winter. Many of the stems also turn a bright rust-red in the fall.

If you peel the green outer layer of the stem, just as you'd pull a zipper, you'll find a center core of white pith. Years ago, this was dried, tied with others, soaked in kitchen grease, and then lighted for rush candles. The pith was also used alone for candle wicks.

Spiral Rush, *Juncus effusus* 'Spirilis' (USDA Zone 4), up to 18 inches tall.
A fantastic cultivar, the Spiral Rush is just what its namesake describes. The living and green corkscrews fall gently to the ground and twist their way in all directions. Besides the garden, the Spiral Rush does well in a pot. Remember to keep the pot in a saucer of water.

Other cultivars of the Common Rush are:
Juncus effusus 'Aureus Striatus' with its stems banded with yellow-green.
Juncus effusus 'Zebrinus' with stems widely banded with greenish-white.
Juncus effusus 'Vittatus' with stems narrowly banded with pure white.

The Sedges and Rushes **83**

Woodrushes comprise a small genus, *Luzula*, of the Juncaceae. Its Latin name is particularly poetic, for it means *luciola*, or glow-worm, referring to the sparkling dew that adheres to the tiny hairs that surmount the stems and leaves. The woodrushes prefer a dry, acid soil located in partial shade. These are originally plants of the woods.

Great Woodrush, *Luzula sylvatica* (USDA Zone 5), up to 12 inches tall.
The Woodrushes have light green leaves that are long, broad, and taper to a point. The plants are fringed with long, white hairs and bloom with a panicle of brownish flowers with yellow stamens in early spring.

Luzula nivea has leaves up to eighteen inches in height with flowering stems of two feet that bear a panicle of small white flowers.

Luzula nivea 'Marginata' is a cultivar that bears cream-colored margins on the leaves.

The Typhaceae family have only one genus, *Typha*, a Greek word for swamp. When I began research on this book and was ordering plants from England, I noticed a listing for Reed Mace, *Typha angustifolia*. It was described as "slender, graceful green leaves up to 1/3 in. across; dark brown "pokers" ¼ in. thick in July. Best in damp soil or water to 6 inches." Apparently a mental image never materialized in my head as I added this plant to the order. Well, imagine my chagrin when I realized that the Reed Mace was the same as our Common Cattail (giving a good case for the use of scientific names, by the by).

They are beautiful and Japanese looking, naturalized in a pool or water garden, but they must be contained if their spreading will cause a problem. The male flowers are on the upper side of the brown pokers and usually disappear before the spikes mature and split, sending the fluffy seeds out on the winds.

To prevent the pokers from breaking open, pick the stems early in the season and hang upside down to dry out.

A charming miniature called *Typha minima*, with leaves to eighteen inches, is often offered in English catalogs.

The Reed Mace has a large and colorful economic history: Flour has been made from the pollen; the stems and leaves are excellent for thatching; and the pollen has occasionally been utilized by fireworks manufacturers, as it's inflammable. In addition, the Russians once treated dysentery with the roots, and country people have used it for years to fill pillows.

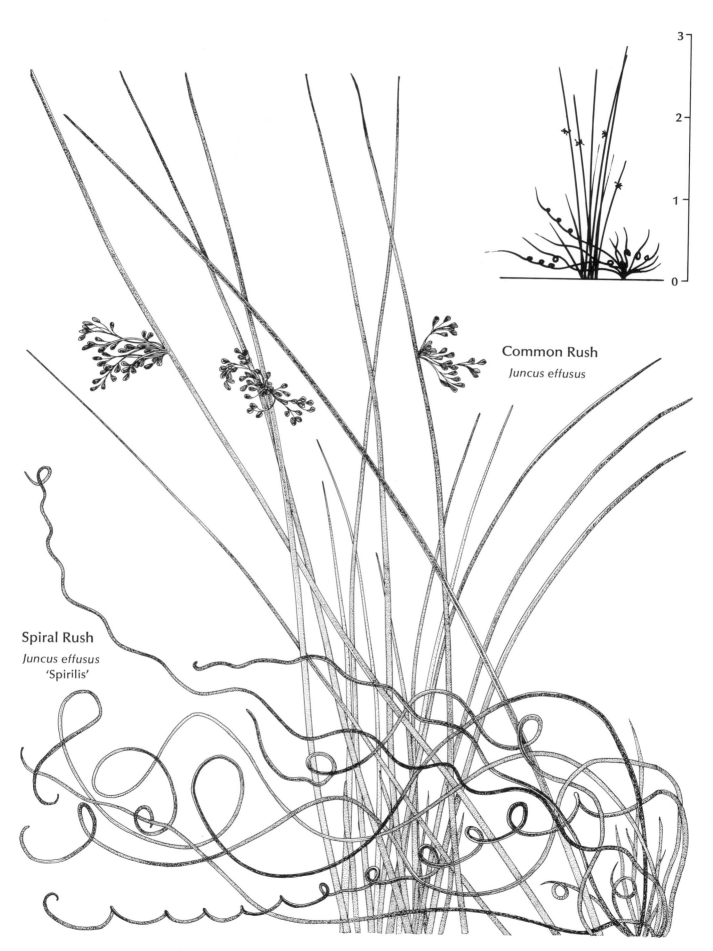

Common Rush
Juncus effusus

Spiral Rush
Juncus effusus
'Spirilis'

3

2

1

0

Common Cattail

Typha angustifolia

5

4

3

2

1

0

5 Plants that Look Like Grasses

. . . SUMMER BLESSED EARTH'S BOSOM BARE
WITH YELLOW DOTS OF GOLD-STAR GRASS,
AND GREY-BLACK SEEDS OF JOB, ENTWINED . . .
—W. S. Lecherś, *Garden Almanac*

Here is a completely arbitrary selection of plants. Most of them are usually thought of as belonging to the grass family, while a few only bear a superficial resemblance. Nevertheless they all share a common trait: they have completely captured my interest.

Sweet Flag or Beewort, *Acorus calamus* (USDA Zone 5), 2-6 feet tall.
As mentioned before, when a plant has wide uses or considerable notoriety, it will bear a great many popular names. Sweet Flag is also known as Myrtle-Flag, Myrtle-Sedge, Myrtle-Grass, Sedge-Grass, Sedge-Cane, Sea-Sedge, Sweet-Myrtle, and Sedge-Root. Part of the reason lies in its value as a source of the drug calamus. Tracking down the spread of this plant is a classic detective story. It was originally known in Europe only as a drug imported from the East until the plant was brought to Europe in 1557 by a Flemish diplomat for Emperor Ferdinand I. By the end of the sixteenth century, Sweet Flag was growing in most European gardens and by the seventeenth century had been brought to America. The plant in its original habitat will not only flower, but bear fruit. However, the one the Flemish diplomat brought to Europe was a variety that did not set fruit. Because of this, none of these plants in Europe or Eastern America set fruit either; but the Sweet Flag of the northern interior of the United States will set fruit, because it is native to the region and not the European clone.

Calamus imparts a pleasant smell to all parts of the Sweet Flag, and when crushed in the fingers has a pungent, bitter taste. It has been used since the days of early Greece for diseases of the eye; and supposedly sailors would chew the root to relieve flatulence and toothache, a deadly combination. The American Indians prized it as a medicine, and even hair tonic has benefitted from its scent.

Acorus calamus is just too large for small fiberglass garden pools but an excellent choice for the larger water garden or a bog garden. While it's possible to grow in a large pot (as *Papyrus*), it's a bit easier to plant in a permanent position, where it will receive full sun.

Acorus calamus 'Variegatus' is much more attractive than the common variety, as the creamish-white and green variegations really add snap to the plant. The requirements are the same, and the sweet odor is still present.

Grassy-leaved Sweet Flag, *Acorus gramineus* (USDA Zone 6), to 12 inches.
This is a small species with slender grasslike leaves that form compact tufts. It is usually grown at the edge of ponds. Although it's called the Sweet Flag, the leaves lack the calamus attributes. An original import from Japan, there is a sculptural look to its form, even if tiny, so try a plant in a small pot, keeping the earth just damp. Protect from the summer sun at noon.

Dwarf Sweet Flag, *Acorus gramineus* 'Pusillus'
(USDA Zone 6), to 6 inches tall.
Dwarf Sweet Flag is a cultivar of the grassy-leaved variety and another Japanese plant, used for pool edgings and even aquariums.

Japanese or Miniature Sweet Flag, *Acorus gramineus variegatus*
(USDA Zone 6), 6-12 inches tall.
This is the most popular of all the *Acorus* and has been used as a house plant for many years. The flat, tough leaves are striped with light-green and white and arrange themselves like miniature folding fans. It's marvelous as an addition to a dish garden and outdoors at the edge of a water garden. Like most variegated plants, give it some protection from the hot summer sun. If too dry, the leaf edges quickly turn brown. This plant is also susceptible to spider mite, so if your specimen is indoors, check it on occasion.

Flowering Rush, *Butomus umbellatus* (USDA Zone 5), 2-4 feet tall.
The only species of *Butomus* (which means *bous*, an ox, and *temno*, cut, referring to the supposition that animals will cut their mouths on the sharp leaves) is *umbellatus*. Originally an import from Asia and England, by 1913 it had naturalized around the St. Lawrence River in Canada. It's easy to grow, and the straplike leaves will make handsome reflections in a water garden. The umbels of six-petaled, pink flowers are a welcome addition. This plant can be naturalized or grown in pots, as with *Papyrus*. In addition, *Butomus* is often naturalized at the edges of lakes and ponds to provide added food for migrating waterfowl. The baked roots are said to be used as food in Asia.

Grass Palm, *Cordyline australis* (USDA Zone 10), up to 40 feet tall.
Every year in late spring, garden centers, especially if near cemeteries, offer pots of plants loosely termed "a decorative arrangement" that contain a geranium (usually zonal), a bit of ivy, and a green rosette of large, grasslike leaves stuck exactly in the center of the pot. The leaves are tapered, about a half-inch in width, and a foot long. It's hard to believe that this "grass" is, in reality, a seedling of *Cordyline australis* and eventually becomes a forty-foot tree in its native New Zealand.

If you keep the seedling and bring it indoors for a house plant, the green rosette will soon "grow a trunk," and after a few years you will have a six- to seven-foot high Grass-Palm with a stout trunk and leaves over two-feet long.

This plant responds to root pruning, so if pot-bound, trim the roots back and hold up on repotting for one more season.

Corn Plant, *Dracaena fragrens massangeana* (USDA Zone 10), up to 15 feet.
When the house-plant boom began, every supermarket and chain store boasted a few of these plants in six-inch pots with a few clumps of heartleaf philodendron twining the plant's trunk. It certainly looks like a corn with its long and shiny leaves banded with yellow and green stripes. In reality these plants are members of the Lily Family and were well-adapted to life in the average home before the energy crisis; they like warm surroundings, and a cool draught will cause the leaves to brown.

Two other members of the *Dracaena* genus are both house plants and excellent for low-level light in office buildings and hotel lobbies: Striped Dracaena (*Dracaena deremensis* 'Warneckei') eventually grows to fifteen feet, has fresh-green leaves with a white band on either side and a streak of milky-green in the center, and until this plant reaches maturity, it's easily mistaken for corn; Ribbon Plant (*Dracaena sanderiana*) has narrow and lanceolate shiny leaves with broad to narrow edgings of white or yellowish white, and like the others, is tolerant of most neglect, except for lack of warmth.

Sweet Flag
Acorus Calamus

6
5
4
3
2
1
0

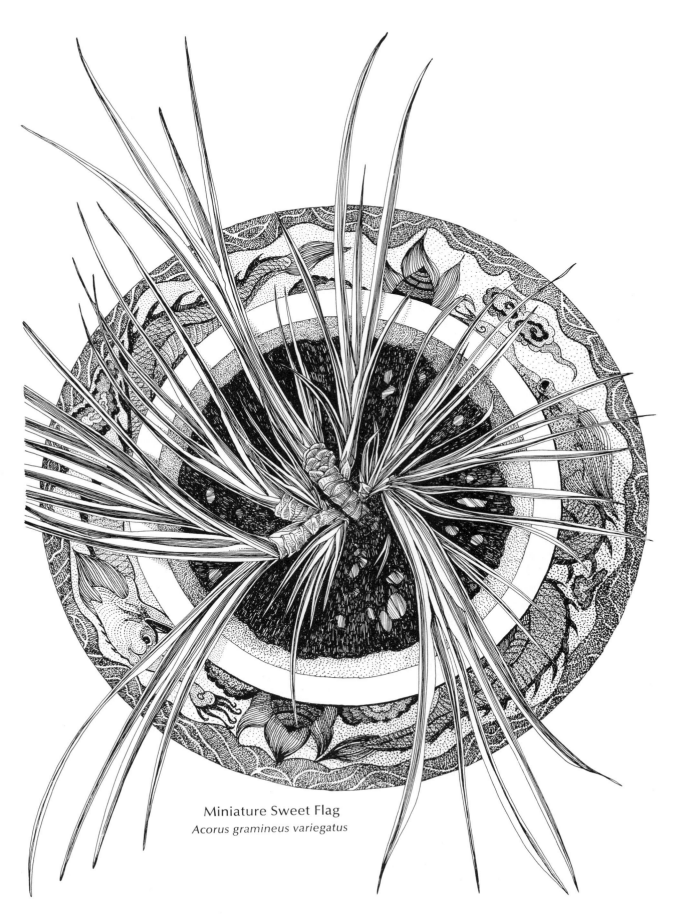

Miniature Sweet Flag
Acorus gramineus variegatus

Flowering Rush
Butomus umbellatus

4

3

2

1

0

Sedge-like Equisetum, *Equisetum scirpoides* (USDA Zone 5), 4-6 inches tall.
Unlike its twenty-foot fossil relatives, or its six- to twelve-foot relatives of today, the Sedge-like Equisetum is so small as to be easily overlooked. The plant is found naturally from Labrador to Pennsylvania, across to Illinois, and then north to British Columbia. Look for it on mossy banks on the edge of woods and, amazingly enough, on the shoulders of country roads, where it grows in such profusion that the tiny plants resemble a miniature field of spring grasses, seemingly impervious to the leftover salts of the winter road crews.

When the plant is examined closely, you'll see that it's not a grass or sedge but a true horsetail, obvious because of its structure of individual, hollow pieces of stem. This is a beautiful and carefree plant for the woodland garden and does quite well in a tiny clay pot, as long as the dirt is constantly moist. Watch it carefully, as this plant can dry out very quickly.

Gold-Star-Grass, *Hypoxis hirsuta* (USDA Zone 5), 8-12 inches tall.
This charming member of the Daffodil Family (Amaryllidaceae) has only one species common to the northeast. *Hypoxis* grows from a small bulblike corm, forming a small and neat tuft of grassy leaves that are called "hirsute" since they bear a covering of sparse but long and thin hairs. The flowers appear in false umbels, each a perfect six-pointed star in a very bright golden-yellow.

Hypoxis prefers a moist soil with some shade from the glare of the hot sun of summer afternoon. Since the plants are small, they look best when naturalized in large colonies.

Bebe Miles credits *Hypoxis* as being one of the longest flowering plants in the outdoor garden.

Propagate by seeds or division of the offsets that will be produced by the corms in the fall.

It is suggested that you try to buy these plants from a local source if your winters are severe, so that the corms can become acclimated.

Blue-Eyed-Grass, *Sisyrinchium angustifolium*
                  (USDA Zone 4), 10-12 inches tall.
The Blue-Eyed-Grasses form a large genus of plants found growing across the United States. At first glance they seem to be grasses that have suddenly learned the trick of producing flowers, but after investigation, they turn out to belong to the Iris Family. Even their common name is misleading, since the flowers are not always blue. These plants are found growing wild, especially in damp soil that is fully exposed to the summer sun. A walk through the country fields of summer will usually turn up a few plants. They certainly deserve a better press, but since the flowers last only until late afternoon, and are never showy in the popular sense, the typical sophisticated gardener has passed them by. But remember, like the Daylily, another day brings another flower, and the grassy foliage should ensure their continued use.

These plants look best in large groups in a naturalized area. They sow easily by seed and can be divided almost any time in the garden year.

The flowers are followed by small, round, black fruits.

The following species are usually available from specialists:
Sisyrinchium angustifolium 'Album' has white flowers.
Sisyrinchium californicum is a Golden-Star species, hardy to USDA Zone 8, and found in the far west.
Sisyrinchium Douglasi has much larger flowers than the eastern species and of a deeper color. Hardy in the northeast, but the leaves disappear after flowering.
Sisyrinchium mucronatum 'Album' a white-flowered form that has threadlike stems with very thin leaves.

Gold-Star-Grass
Hypoxis hirsuta

Blue-Eyed-Grass
Sisyrinchium angustifolium

Blue Lily Turf, *Liriope Muscari* (USDA Zone 6), 12-18 inches tall.
The Lily Turfs, as their common name implies, are grasslike members of the Lily Family. They are native to Japan and China. Generally used as groundcovers, the Lily Turfs spread easily with a network of rhizomes and tolerate both sun and shade. They are hardy in USDA Zone 6 if some protection is given against truly bitter winds by either snow cover or a winter mulch. In addition to their attractive foliage and habit, *Liriope* flower with a terminal spike of waxy blooms. They are propagated by seed or division.

These plants also make excellent pot plants. Keep the well-drained soil mix evenly moist; move the plants from rooms that are too warm; and keep them out of extremely hot sunlight or the leaves will quickly turn brown.

There are three cultivars of *Liriope*:
Liriope Muscari 'Grandiflora' bears light, lavender flowers.
Liriope Muscari 'Munroe White' needs shade and bears white flowers.
Liriope Muscari 'Variegata' has flowers that are a dark violet. Its leaves are a light-green striped with white, although they revert to green with age.

In addition, another species, *Liriope spicata*, is described as having grasslike leaves up to seventeen inches long on a plant only ten inches high, so that the leaves creep along the ground. Flowers on this species are pale violet to white, and its common name is Creeping Lily Turf.

Mondo Grass, *Ophiopogon Jaburan* (USDA Zone 8), 8-12 inches tall.
Mondo Grass is a member of a family of sod-forming perennial herbs originally from Korea and Japan. Like *Liriope*, they are lilies and very valuable as groundcovers in milder climates. Mondo Grass is so undemanding that it makes a perfect house plant, tolerating almost as much neglect as the Aspidistra (and they are related). In colder climates, Mondo can be used in pots on a terrace or deck for the entire summer and brought inside to use again. Keep the well-drained soil evenly moist, provide moderate temperatures, and protect from a too-hot sun. The plants bloom with drooping clusters of tiny, nodding flowers, usually white. They produce dark blue fruits. *Ophiopogon Jaburan* 'Variegatus' is an often available cultivar that has white stripes on the leaves.

Dwarf Mondo Grass, *Ophiopogon japonicus*
              (USDA Zone 8), up to 8 inches tall.
Also called Snakebeard, this grasslike plant is a smaller species that has tuberous roots. Its leaves grow up to fifteen inches long, and are a very dark green. The flowers are a light lilac to white. This plant makes a good choice for edging in a warm greenhouse.

Black Mondo Grass, *Ophiopogon planiscapus* 'Arabicus' is a cultivar with very linear leaves up to twenty inches long. With age, the leaves turn a deep purple-black color, making a most unusual statement for a house plant. The blossoms are pink, and the fruits are a bluish-green.

New Zealand Flax, *Phormium tenax* (USDA Zone 9), up to 3-4 feet tall.
While only a warm climate is hospitable for Flax, it is an excellent container plant for pot gardens on the terrace or porch. *Tenax* and its cultivars form most attractive shapes with their fanlike leaves. These stiff and leathery swords split at the tip of the leaf, and it's a temptation to pull the strands that are the flax fibers used in textiles. Keep the soil evenly moist, and give the plants hot sun. If they do well, you'll have to divide them every three or four years.

Blue Lily Turf

Liriope Muscari

Mondo Grass
Ophiopogon jaburan

Phormium tenax 'Atropurpureum' has reddish-purple leaves.

Phorimum tenax 'Rubrum' produces red leaves.

Phorimum tenax 'Variegatum' has variegated leaves striped with creamy-yellow and white.

Flowers are in racemes and are red or yellow in color.

If you cannot locate any of these plants, seeds are available both from America and England.

Fan-Grass, *Reineckia gracilis*, (USDA Zone 9), up to 8-16 inches tall.

Fan-Grass is another grasslike plant that belongs to the Lily Family and is only used out-of-doors in very warm climates. Here, in the north, this is an excellent pot plant. The narrow green leaves are thin, tough, leathery, and about one-half-inch wide. They curve in elegant arches starting from the base and are arranged in groups of two. The flowers are fragrant and pink, appearing on densely packed spikes, and are followed by red fruits.

Plant Fan-Grass in a well-drained soil kept evenly moist, and give it partial shade. As for most house plants, a cool room is preferable.

Eel-Grass, *Vallisneria spiralis*, leaves up to 6 feet long.

Any aquarium hobbyist is familiar with Eel-Grass. It is a genus with only two species, *spiralis* and *neotropicalis*, both found in the continental United States and named after Antonio Vallisneria, an Italian naturalist of the eighteenth century. It is usually mistaken for underwater grass until its white blossoms appear at the water's surface. In quiet ponds, these plants can form veritable forests, providing food and cover for both animal and waterfowl, not to mention fish.

In outdoor ornamental ponds and pools, Eel-Grass should be set directly in soil or prepotted, as with *Papyrus*. They then provide food for goldfish and shade for pool water, preventing undue algal growth.

Bear-Grass, *Xerophyllum asphodeloides* (USDA Zone 5), up to 12 inches tall with flowering stem up to 5 feet.

Turkey-Beard is another name for this lovely plant native to the eastern United States south from the Pine Barrens of New Jersey. If given either snow cover or winter mulch and planted in a protected spot, Bear-Grass will survive Zone 5 winters. The stiff and grassy leaves grow from a thick root-stock and are generally 6-8 inches long. Their neat and compact growth looks especially well when plants are grown in colonies, when they closely resemble the Fescues.

The surprise, though, is the flowering habit. From May to July, as the world warms for summer, a 2-5 foot stem arises from the center of the grassy clump, bearing at its top a large and dense raceme of tiny, white flowers.

When planting Bear-Grass, use only small plants, since the genus has very deep roots that are easily destroyed with careless digging. Make frequent waterings until plants are well-established. Use rich, rocky soil that has perfect drainage, and try for a woodland setting. Only mature plants will flower, so be patient. But remember—it's worth the wait.

Yellow-Eyed-Grass, *Xyris torta* (USDA Zone 5), up to 10-18 inches tall.

This is the Yellow-Eyed-Grasses' one representative in the northern United States. The rest of the tribe are at home in the southern states. Flowers resemble three-petaled buttercups and emerge one or two at a time from a scaled spike that looks just like a miniature pinecone. While the flowers are small and soon wither, a grouping of the plants provides a yellow cloud of blossoms.

Bear-Grass

Xerophyllum asphodeloides

The narrow leaves grow in a fan-shaped cluster and when not in bloom are usually mistaken for grass. The plants prefer a damp and protected location. In the southernmost states they will bloom throughout the year.

Xyris baldwiniana has clusters of threadlike leaves up to twelve inches long, forming large clumps of flowering stems bearing large flowers on small cones.

Xyris fimbriata is the largest species and has leaves over two feet long.

Xyris platylepis has twisted leaves that reach twenty inches on twisted flowering stems, all arising from a bulbous base.

Strange as it may seem, the closest floral relatives to the *Xyris* genus are the Bromeliad Family of pineapple fame.

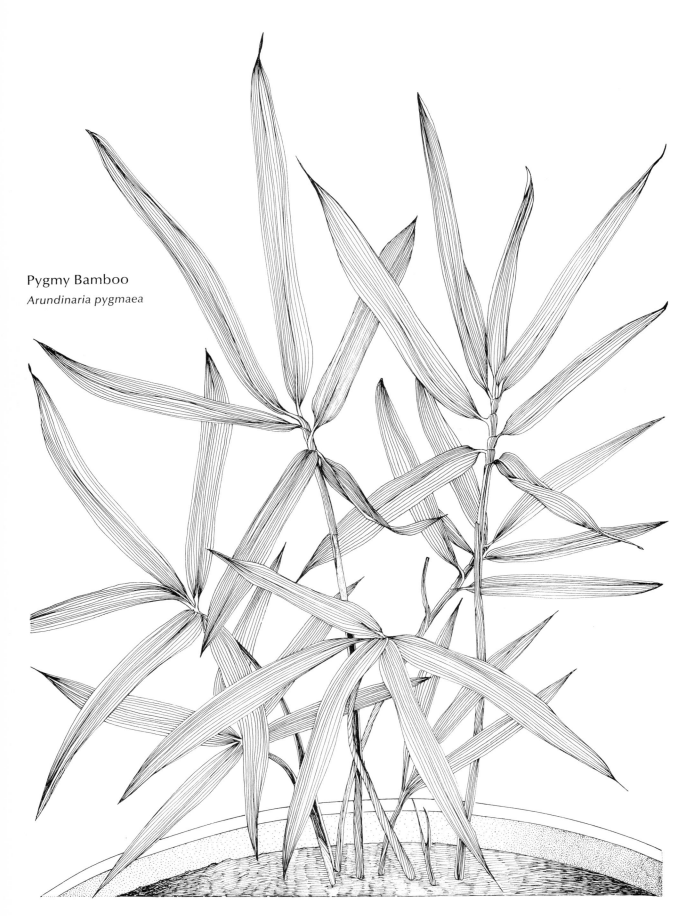

Pygmy Bamboo
Arundinaria pygmaea

6 The Bamboos

*. . . AND WHEN WE MARRY, HAPPY WE'LL BE,
UNDER THE BAMBOO, UNDERNEATH THE BAMBOO TREE.*
—Old popular song

For me, the bamboos conjure up visions of steamy jungles with orange orangutans crawling beneath masses of dark-green leaves, or Chinese robber barons at war with Malayan rubber pirates, or even oriental brushes producing placid pictures, but never suburban New Jersey, New York City, or gardens of New England. However, many of the ornamental bamboos are hardy in USDA Zone 4, with protection, and their uses in the northern landscape have been largely overlooked. If you live in an area too cold for the hardier bamboos, there are many species that do extremely well in tubs and containers. For those so inclined, you can even *bonsai* bamboos.

Most Americans think of fishing poles when the subject of bamboo is brought up. Then someone always counters with the fact that fiberglass rods are used today, unless there is a true fly-fisherman in the group, who will immediately inform all that the best poles in the world are still handcrafted with Chinese bamboo but are so expensive as to be priced out of reach. In the past, Thomas Edison used bamboo filaments in the first light bulbs.

In the Orient, bamboo has centuries of tradition behind it and has literally served in everything from banquets to buildings. The young sprouts of several species are considered a delicacy, and construction projects, especially in Japan, rely on bamboo scaffolding in lieu of metal. The Chinese, not to be outdone, have used pulped bamboo as a major source of paper for centuries.

All the continents except Europe have native bamboos. Here in America we have the Giant Southern Cane (*Arundinaria gigantea*), which grows from southern Ohio to Oklahoma and then south to the Gulf, and a subspecies, Switchcane (*Arundinaria tecta*), which grows along the Atlantic coast south from Maryland.

For many years our native bamboos were listed as giant grasses. Just what is the difference between the two? To begin with, the differences are ones of quality not quantity, as both share the same structural elements, although bamboos are a bit more primitive, in the evolutionary sense.

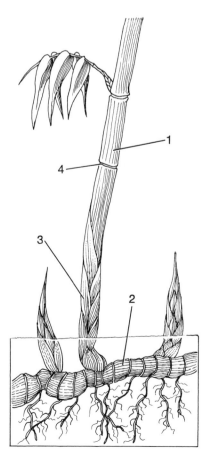

The *culms* (1) or stems are very woody and are extensions of a complex and well-developed system of *rhizomes* (2). A *culm sheath* (3) is often found covering the stem as it leaves the ground, and a pronounced *culm node* (4) that corresponds to the knot on a grass stem is a distinctive feature. In addition, there are many "not-so-obvious" differences in structure of both the plant and the flowers.

Many bamboos are *monocarpic*: they only live a short time after flowering. A few never stop flowering, but the majority fall between these two extremes. The tropical varieties tend to be more monocarpic than those of the north, and, a most interesting fact, all clones of a particular species of bamboo will flower at the same time regardless of where they are in the world.

There are dozens of bamboos offered for cultivation. I've picked fourteen, giving for each cultural instructions, display suggestions, and a USDA Zone number. I have to emphasize that you must try to grow these plants yourself to prove survival in the colder parts of the country. Every piece of property of any size has *microclimates*, areas of perhaps only a few square feet that differ substantially in high and low temperatures from other areas twenty feet away. Microclimates are due to wind patterns, large trees or topography that deflect wind and reflect sunlight, for examples, and are often the result of man's creations: e.g. house foundations that leak heat, corners of fences, etc.

Because of these climate variations, a Zone 6 bamboo will often flourish at one end of the block and a Zone 5 variety will perish at the other. Remember, too, that winds are an ever-present danger. A temperature of zero becomes −21°F when the wind blows at just ten miles an hour. At that wind speed, the leaves stir and you feel wind on your face, but the medium-sized branches on a tree do not even move! If your area is short on snow in the winter, always use a winter mulch to protect from sudden changes in freeze to thaw that will actually thrust plants from the ground and tear their roots.

Finally, never leave any plant, bamboo or otherwise, outside in cold weather in an unprotected tub or container.

Pygmy Bamboo, *Arundinaria pygmaea* (USDA Zone 7), up to 8-10 inches tall.
This is the smallest of the bamboos. In addition to making an excellent groundcover (which can be cut by a mower if it spreads), it's also at home in a pot as a house plant. As with most bamboos, it likes full sun and a moist, well-drained soil. Remember to fertilize on a regular schedule, as bamboos are heavy feeders. Apply either a lawn or garden fertilizer once a month during active growth.

Variegated Pygmy Bamboo, *Arundinaria pygmaea* 'Variegated'
(USDA Zone 7), up to 16 inches tall.
A cream- and white-striped cultivar of the Pygmy Bamboo, that in addition to being another excellent groundcover makes one of the most desirable house plants in the bamboo category. When living in a pot, the plant becomes a full clump of lovely foliage that prefers good light and evenly moist soil. Like most variegated plants, this can take a location of open shade. If grown outdoors, give plenty of cover if temperatures go below 0°F.

Arundinaria Simonii var. *variegata* (USDA Zone 7), up to 20 feet tall.
This is the variegated form of the Simon Bamboo. It is most unusual in that the variegated leaves will appear mixed with plain green on the same plant. The white-striped leaves are always slightly narrower. This bamboo was originally imported from China by way of Europe and has been a popular ornamental for years. It is excellent for producing a screen or hedge, and while not economical for commercial use, the new shoots are edible. During the Second World War, an American concern grew and marketed the culms as handles for the mallets used in shuffleboard. It makes a reasonable house plant, but is not as attractive to me when small enough to be allowed in the home.

Arundinaria viridistriata (USDA Zone 7), up to 30-36 inches tall.
Sometimes sold as *Phyllostachys argentea* and called the Kamuro-zasa Bamboo, this is a true beauty whether for outdoor planting (where it should have a metal guard beneath the soil, as it is ruggedly invasive) or in a planter or a tub. The leaves are hard to describe; they have a velvety look when new, and the golden and green tones meld together from a distance. This species needs partial shade when out-of-doors, and, if grown in pots, needs well-drained soil.

Make sure that you protect them with a winter mulch in colder areas. If brought indoors for the winter, this bamboo prefers a cool room temperature.

Variegated Pygmy Bamboo

Arundinaria pygmaea
'Variegated'

*Arundinaria
Simonii variegata*

Arundinaria viridistriata

Beechey Bamboo, *Bambusa Beecheyana* (USDA Zone 9), up to 50 feet tall.
The *Bambusa* genus of bamboos comes primarily from the warmer regions of Asia, where many of them are harvested for timber, paper manufacture, and food. The Beechy Bamboo, named after the British naval officer who explored the Pacific, makes a beautiful ornamental with its bright green culms that grow to a four-inch diameter and gracefully arch with age. The dark green leaves are ten inches long and two inches wide. The Beechey Bamboo is one of the primary sources of edible bamboo shoots in China and many other parts of the world. Like most bamboos, this will do well in a large tub if given a cool position, excellent light, and fresh air. Bamboos suffer when kept any place without adequate movement of air.

Fernleaf Bamboo, *Bambusa multiplex* 'Fernleaf'
(USDA Zone 9), up to 15 feet tall.
Also called the Ornamental Hedge Bamboo, the Fernleaf varieties usually grow from seven to ten feet tall on reedlike stems with leaves one-quarter inch wide by one and one-half inches long. This plant needs plenty of water to hold the foliage but may be enjoyed indoors in cool, bright rooms for long periods. Under too many unpleasant conditions, it will lose the fernleaf character and revert to its typical form where the leaves are much larger and on longer stems.

These bamboos are of Chinese origin, and the parent species (*Bambusa multiplex*) has been used to provide timbers for low-cost housing and fiber for paper-pulp.

Buddha's-Belly Bamboo, *Bambusa ventricosa*
(USDA Zone 9), up to 15-50 feet tall.
Buddha's-Belly is a clump-forming bamboo that is grown in tubs with purposely dry and poor soil where it is also allowed to become root-bound. At this time, the spaces between the nodes on the culms become swollen and look like many tiny, well-fed stomachs. When grown under proper conditions, the swellings stretch, and eventually the stems become straight. All over the Orient it is prized as a container plant and grown for its unusual stem shape when deprived of sustenance.

The Giant Bamboo, *Dendrocalamus giganteus*
(USDA Zone 10), up to over 100 feet tall.
The largest of all the bamboos, the Giant Bamboo originally came from Java. It will grow up to 120 feet high with culms over a foot in diameter. The nodes on the culms are up to sixteen inches apart, and twenty-inch leaves are borne in arched masses toward the tops of the stems. A silhouette of this bamboo looks a great deal like an atomic bomb explosion. It needs water, warm temperatures, and plenty of sun. In the Orient it is often used for construction scaffolding, and sections of the culm are large enough to serve as water buckets. Since the culms can grow as fast as a foot a day, they were reportedly used to torture prisoners-of-war during World War II by tying men to the ground in bamboo groves.

Yellowgrove Bamboo, *Phyllostachys aureosulcata*
(USDA Zone 6), up to 30 feet tall.
This is the hardiest of the bamboos and will withstand temperatures up to −20°F with adequate protection. The grooves between the nodes on the green culms are yellowish. Young sprouts in early spring are edible.

Black Bamboo, *Phyllostachys nigra* (USDA Zone 7), up to 25 feet tall.
Although it sounds like a cliché, this plant is deservedly called the "Jewel of the Bamboos" with its bright green leaves and jet black culms. Originally from Southern China, the Black Bamboo will reach a height of twenty-five feet when out-of-doors but usually stops at about ten feet when grown in containers. It needs good light but prefers some shade from very hot afternoon sun. When new, the culms are green and speckled with black, but they become solid black with age. The shoots which appear at mid-spring are edible.

Even when small, this bamboo is a beautiful plant and has held its leaves for me for several years, even as a well-confined houseplant.

Sasa veitchii (USDA Zone 9), up to 5 feet tall.
The *Sasa* genus is mostly from Japan and is rarely tall. This species, sometimes called the Kuma Bamboo Grass, has leaves up to eight inches long and one and one-half inches wide that are a very bright green. In the fall, these leaves develop a straw-colored margin that is applied so evenly that it looks like the work of little elves. This quality gives it additional interest for the winter garden. It makes a good groundcover and grows well in pots and containers.

Semiarundinaria fastuosa (USDA Zone 8), up to 25 feet tall.
There are three species of this bamboo from Japan and Eastern Asia, where they are extensively used for garden ornamentals. The dark green culms have purplish-brown stems with seven-inch leaf blades. Since the rhizomes spread slowly, they are often used for hedges.

Shibatea Kumasaca (USDA Zone 8), up to 6 feet tall.
Often sold as *Sasa Kumasaca,* this is one of two species of small bamboos, one from China and this one from Japan. It's a good container plant and spreads slowly. My example was potted and then put in one of the decorative wicker baskets that are now being exported from Mainland China. It is said to be partial to acidic soils; alkaline soils will cause leaf burn, and leaf damage occurs at temperatures below 10°F.

Heavenly Bamboo, *Nadina domestica* (USDA Zone 6), up to 8 feet.
It seems fitting that the final bamboo selection, although called "heavenly" and originally from China and Japan, is not a bamboo at all but a member of the Barberry family. It's an attractive, low-growing shrub that will grow up to eight feet tall in good conditions. The canelike stems are a reddish-brown, and the leaves are pinkish when new, turning a light fresh green when mature. Its lacey foliage is very reminiscent of bamboo. Flowers appear in long panicles followed by red berries (a cultivar 'Alba' has white berries), and the plants are usually propagated by seed. In the fall, the leaves will turn a brilliant red and stay on the plant until the winds blow them away.

When grown as a house plant, use well-drained soil, kept evenly moist, with lots of sun and a cool room.

Heavenly Bamboo will grow to full maturity in USDA Zone 7, but the roots are hardy in Zone 6 if given sensible winter protection.

Black Bamboo

Phyllostachys nigra

etc
10
9
8
7
6
5
4
3
2
1
0

Shibatea Kumasaca

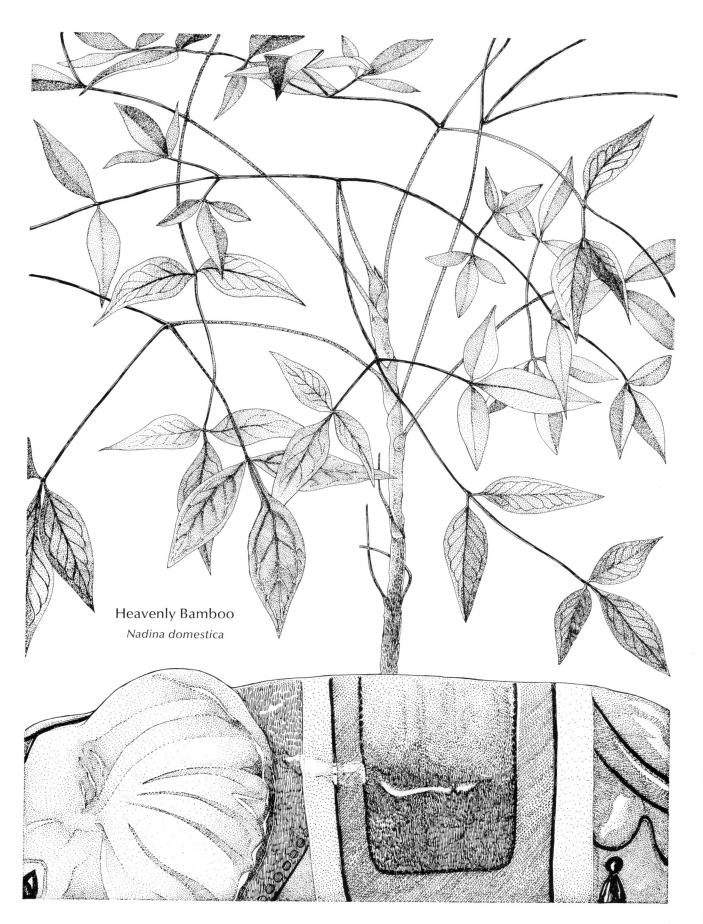

Heavenly Bamboo
Nadina domestica

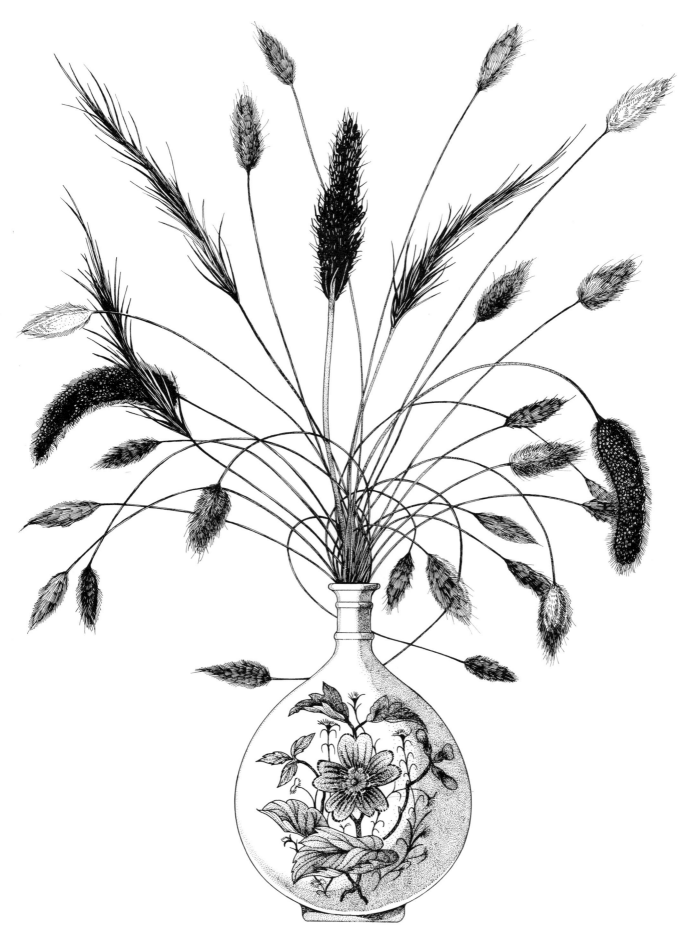

Dried Grasses for Decoration

THOUGH NOTHING CAN BRING BACK THE HOUR
OF SPLENDOUR IN THE GRASS, OF GLORY IN THE FLOWER;
—Wordsworth, *Intimations of Immortality*

Decorating the home and office with dried grasses (and flowers) is an old, old practice accomplished with varying degrees of success and good taste. Since most of my time is devoted to living plants (and, on occasion, those that have cast-off parts that continue to be attractive), my color sense has become imbued with the natural tints of nature. I must confess that I have no patience with the art of dyeing (in contrast to drying) plants as usually practiced today.

Centuries ago, the available dyes were of natural origin, *i.e.* they were produced by living things, mostly plants. Then came the Victorians, who, never to be outdone by nature, developed an array of dyes with brilliant colors based on a new chemistry of coal-tar derivatives. When the Victorian dyes are viewed today in pressed flower paintings or glassed-in bouquets of the period, exposure to light and air over many years have mellowed and muted the colors, but if seen in their pristine intensity, they would knock your eyes out. (We should remember that they had no bright or fluorescent lights, and the sun was kept out by heavy drapes to prevent fabric from fading, so pressure was strong to make the colors unnaturally bright.) I abhor the artificial colors of today with their vermillion, green, purple, and, of all things, turquoise tints, and find them double damned when placed on dried plants.

So if you wish to learn of the art of dyeing, you must search elsewhere; but, if you are interested in the art of drying—drying grasses in their natural majesty—then read on. It's a remarkably simple process.

The only equipment needed are wire coat-hangers, paper twistems left over from plastic bags, and a sharp knife or scissors.

Gather the grasses in mid-afternoon on a dry and sunny day, after the dews of morning have evaporated and before the afternoon damp sets in. Pick stems with blossoms that are not yet completely open, and cut the stems as long as you can; it's much easier to trim stems for a shorter arrangement than glue stems back together for length. Strip any excess leaves from the stem; these will only shrivel into unattractiveness during the drying process, leaving only the seed heads and panicles. Tie small bunches of stems together, enabling air to pass easily between each stem, and hang them upside down on wire coat-hangers, again allowing plenty of room between bunches. Then hang the hangers well apart in a basement room or garage that is cool, dry, dark, and airy. The cool temperature prevents the plant sap from drying too quickly and forcing the spikelets to go to seed; the dry and airy atmosphere prevents the formation of mold and mildew; and the darkness prevents premature fading of the floral parts.

Check your bundles every few days, since the stems shrink as they dry, and many could fall to the floor and be ruined.

Most of the straight grasses should be dried in this manner. Those like the Foxtails, which benefit from a curved stem, should be staked in a dry vase or container and kept upright but stored with the others.

Many of the leaves of grasses, especially the Reeds and the *Miscanthus* species, are excellent additions to dried arrangements, so be sure to include some of them.

With very delicate seedheads like Cloud Grass and Champagne Grass, a very light spray with liquid hair-net is often beneficial in holding them together.

Be sure and pick enough grasses for your bouquets. In order to be really effective, the flowerheads should be massed.

Generally, your grasses will be ready for arrangements in two weeks to a month.

Arrangement of flowers, whether fresh or dried, is a matter of personal taste, but a few general rules could be followed to advantage:

1. Use natural materials for containers, like stoneware crocks, jugs, and even wicker baskets. In essence you are trying to match textures, and dried grasses would be a bit out of place in a highly patterned Sèvres porcelain pitcher or vase.

2. Always think of scale. Ordinarily you would not take five Cat-tails and use them with one piece of Cloud Grass, as one would completely overcome the other. However, if you massed thirty stems of Cloud Grass together, the massive visual impact would work harmoniously with Cat-tails.

3. Avoid the obvious. Driftwood is great on beaches, and even has a place in many decorative themes, but unless you come up with a unique way of using it, it will detract from most dried flower arrangements.

4. Consider the background. If you can change the lighting arrangements at will in your home, and if decorating schemes are swept in and out with every new floral arrangement, pay no attention to the following advice: very complicated arrangements should be placed in a position where they have "air to breathe," not pushed into a tight little corner; dark groupings usually look best against lighter walls; light and airy arrangements generally work best with darker backgrounds; and never overlook the effect of light and shadow both on the arrangement and the space behind it.

5. Throw your arrangements out every spring. This saves on dusting (and dust will fall during the winter months) and forces you into new paths of creativity every year.

Remember, too, that these are only suggestions and should not be slavishly followed.

When I was a kid and addicted, like most kids in those days, to Plastic Man, the Green Lantern, and Wonder Woman, the comic books also contained startling, wild, and totally tasteless advertisements with cartoon drawings offering products from itching powder to X-ray binoculars. No doubt an advance indication of my horticultural interests, my favorite was an item called "Grow Hair on Cueball's Head." This last product was a large, hollow, white-clay head with a bald top peppered with tiny holes. You put grass seed on the head, kept the inside filled with water, and Cueball soon began to sprout a new crop. While it is true that I always thought of the grass-growing heads as a novelty of the 40s, I have since learned that Cueball goes back further in time and was created in the 1870s, when the following excerpts about growing grasses in cones was written in a popular gardening book of the era:

Far prettier than many a pretentious and costly ornament is a simple bowl of grasses planted in pine cones, set in sand, in moss, or common soil. If grown in cones—procure them from the woods, and sprinkle in as much soil as their scales will retain; then scatter the grass seeds over it and sprinkle with water; place the cones in sand or moss—and be sure that they do not become dry—but water them sparingly at first, once a day, and set in a moderately warm place. Soon the seeds will sprout, and the tiny spears protrude in every direction.

Grass will sprout and grow in pine cones [*left*] without any soil, but it serves to prevent the cone from closing too tightly when sprinkled, and also makes a more vigorous growth. The cones can be suspended in a window, either singly or in groups of three fastened together with thread wire; or a rustic basket or stand can be procured, and filled with cones with different kinds of grass, growing in each cone. There are three thousand different species of grasses in the world, and their study is a pleasing pursuit.

A very charming effect can be produced by placing a wet sponge in a glass bowl, and sprinkling over it canary seed, grasses and flax seeds; soon it will be covered with a thick growth of fresh bright green; it must be judiciously watered; if kept too dry it will wither away; if too wet it may damp off.

Children and invalids can derive much pleasure from raising a grass garden; it is better to select the dwarf varieties, as the taller kinds require more nourishment. . . .

A Tumbler Garden [*left*] may be made as follows: fill a common tumbler or goblet with water, cut out a round of cotton batting, or of soft thick flannel of just the size to cover the surface, and lay it gently upon the water, upon this scatter the seeds of grass, or flax . . . and gently set the tumbler away in a dark place. In a few days the seed will start . . . [and] begin to penetrate the cotton or flannel, slowly sending down their delicate white fibres to the bottom of the vessel, while the top will be covered with a little thicket of green; after the second day the vessel must be kept in a warm tight place, and two or three times a week carefully replenished with water by means of a teaspoon, or syringe inserted beneath the flannel.

The devices for growing grasses can be extended *ad libitum*, and none are so poor that they cannot secure a tumbler or a saucer garden, which will prove a delight and joy to all beholders, while its care will be of the slightest.*

I shall forego making any comments on the social implications of the above and assume that the reader will find it both useful and informative.

---

*Henry T. Williams, ed. *Window Gardening*, (New York: Ladies Floral Cabinet Company), 1871, 281-83.

Besides the grasses mentioned in Chapters two and three that are usually grown indoors, others such as Bulbous Oat Grass, Purple Moor Grass, the Fescues, most of the sedges, and even some of the smaller annuals such as Cloud Grass can be also used to good advantage as indoor plants. The only thing you need be aware of is the need for good lighting; most of the grasses will either cease to grow or become too straggly under poor light. This means at least six hours a day of direct sunlight. If you are unable to provide such illumination, it's best to grow the grasses out-of-doors. Use a soil mixture of 1/3 potting soil, 1/3 sphagnum peat moss, and 1/3 sand. Fertilize weekly with any standard plant food while the plants are actively growing.

GRASSES IN THE WILD

One of the most enjoyable things about gardening is discovering the beauty of a wild plant that, you think, has escaped notice by anyone else for many years. While many such plants become too weedy and overtake their more civilized cousins who have sacrificed strength for beauty, and are too coarse even for a wild garden, when dried for arrangements their grace and charm is once more visible. The following eight species are found growing around the country either in the fields or by the roadside (illustrations are on pps. 116-17):

1. Cut Grass (*Leersia oryzoides*) is called so because the margins of the leaf blades are covered with sharp little spines thar can catch on skin and clothing, even causing cuts on the hand and arm, so use caution in gathering. It grows on the edge of swamps and easily reaches a height of five feet. The panicles, when carefully dried, are lovely with their shiny black spikelets.

2. Green Foxtail (*Setaria viridis*) looks exactly like its namesake. This is a very common annual grass that becomes a weedy pest to the farmer. It can grow along the graveled soft-shoulder of northern highways, where it's easy to spot but dangerous to gather. Its green color, unlike that of many other grasses, remains after drying.

3. Wild Chess (*Bromus secalinus*) is another annual, weedy grass. Although it does not have the values of other species grown for ornament, it deserves to be used in dried arrangements for its color alone. The Chess Grasses dry to a rich, golden brown color that reminds one of the summer past.

4. Orchard Grass (*Dactylis glomerata*) has a variegated form that is most valuable in gardens. The common species was first introduced in the United States about 1760 and was brought over from Europe, where it was considered to be a most valuable grass. First cultivated in Virginia, it is now found almost everywhere and is grown both for hay and as a forage grass. The plants grow in large tussoks.

5. Velvet Grass (*Holcus lanatus*) has a variegated variety that is used for an ornamental, but the common variety, while once held in high esteem for its hay, is now banished to the weed category, since under some conditions it has been known to kill livestock. Cattle have never been fond of the grass, and in the 1800s the Duke of Bedford, following the sage suggestion of Sir Humphrey Davy, experimented with sprinkling salt over the hay to make it more palatable, but the animals still showed good sense and refused to touch it.

6. Wild Rye (*Elymus villosus*) is a perennial found along stream banks and old roads that wander through moist woods. The leaves are thin and dark, and the upper surfaces are velvety to the touch. Often confused with Bottlebrush, Wild Rye is just a little too weedy looking for the garden, but it is fine in dried arrangements.

7. Wright's Triple-Awned Grass (*Aristida Wrightii*) is a member of the Needle-grass Family, and, as such, is considered to be dangerous for animals because of the sharp awns and the pointed callus of the spikelets, which easily inflict injury. They yield little forage and are usually found on the poorest of soils, especially in the western part of the country. However, they excel when cut and dried for winter display.

8. Smooth Brome Grass (*Bromus inermis*) is a perennial sod grass, native to Europe and China. It was introduced to the United States in 1884 and has since been widely grown as a pasture and hay grass. It frequently escapes from cultivation and grows along roadside ditches and on the edge of fields. The stems grow to a height of three to four feet, and the panicles dry with the gold-brown of all the bromes.

In addition to those pictured, other wild grasses have merit as additions to winter bouquets: Purpletop *(Tridens flavus)* has large and handsome, drooping purple panicles; the Broad-leaved Panic Grasses, particularly *Panicum latifolium* or *Panicum clandestinum* (the word *panic* refers to *panicle*, and not fear) have the odd habit of blooming twice. The second time, the upper joints of the stems fall away and the branches multiply, making it look like a bamboo's foliage.

1   2   3   4   5

6   7   8

APPENDIX A:

Plant and Seed Suppliers

The following companies are by no means the only ones in the world that supply ornamental grasses. If there are others who wish to be listed in the future, kindly notify the publisher.

Applewood Seed Company
833 Parfet Street
Lakewood, Colorado 80215
Free list of seeds.

Corham Artificial Flowers
300 Central Avenue, White Plains, New York 10606
3910 Harry Hines Boulevard, Dallas, Texas 75219
11800 West Olympic, Los Angeles, California 90064
3076 North East 12th Terrace, Fort Lauderdale, Florida 33334
Large collection of dried grasses.

De Giorgi Company, Inc.
Council Bluffs, Iowa 51501
Catalog of flower seeds including many grasses, 50¢.

Garden Place
6780 Heisley Road
Mentor, Ohio 44060
Many ornamental grasses offered in excellent catalog, 50¢.

Hillier & Sons
Winchester SO22 5DN, England
Ordering from Hillier & Sons is an experience worth all. Write first.

C.G. Hollett, Greenbank Nursery
Sedbergh, Cumbria
LA10 5AG, Scotland
Most complete selection of sedges. Write first.

International Growers Exchange
P. O. Box 397
Farmington, Michigan 48024
Catalogs cost $3.00 but cover many nurseries. A number of grasses are offered.

Lafayette Home Nursery
Lafayette, Illinois 61449
Free list of prairie grass and wild flowers.

Logee's Greenhouses
Danielson, Connecticut 06239
Catalog of house plants is $1.00. Includes many grasses and sedges grown in the home.

Mellingers
North Lima, Ohio 44452
Free catalog. Lists bamboos and sometimes grasses from Europe.

Nichol's Garden Nursery
1190 North Pacific Highway
Albany, Oregon 97321
Catalog is 50¢. Supply all kinds of ornamental corns.

Pacific Bamboo Gardens
P. O. Box 16145
San Diego, California 92116
Free list. Catalog with growing instructions is $1.00 and well done. Extensive collection of bamboos.

Palette Gardens
26 West Zion Hill Road
Quakertown, Pennsylvania 18951
Catalog is 50¢. Good supply of ornamental grasses.

Paradise Gardens
14 May Street
Whitman, Massachusetts 02382
Catalog is $1.00. Dealers in aquatics.

Harry E. Saier
Dimondale, Michigan 48821
Free catalog. Some grass seeds.

Park Seed Co., Inc.
Greenwood, South Carolina 29647
Free catalog. Many grass seeds.

Perry's Hardy Plant Farm
Enfield, Middlesex EN2 9BG, England
Large collection of aquatics, including rushes.

Clyde Robin
P. O. Box 2091
Castro Valley, California 94546
Catalog is $1.00. Seeds of wild grasses.

Siskiyou Rare Plant Nursery
522 Franquette Street
Medford, Oregon 97501
Catalog is 50¢. Offer many of the Carex tribe.

Stokes Seeds
Box 548
Buffalo, New York 14240
Catalog is free. Good selection of seeds; their Ornamental Mix is excellent.

Sunnybrook Farms Nursery
9445 Mayfield Road
Chesterland, Ohio 44026
Good selection of grass plants, but they do not ship.

Thompson & Morgan
P. O. Box 24
401 Kennedy Boulevard
Somerdale, New Jersey 08083
Catalog is free and mouth-watering. Large selection of grass seeds.

William Tricker, Inc.
74 Allendale Avenue, Saddle River, New Jersey 07458
7125 Tanglewood Drive, Independence, Ohio 44131
Catalog is 25¢. Dealers in aquatics.

Van Ness Water Gardens
2460 North Euclid Avenue
Upland, California 91786
Catalog is 50¢.

Martin Viette Nurseries
Northern Boulevard (25A)
Muttontown, Long Island, New York 11732
Catalog is $1.50. No mail orders but a good selection of grasses for motoring New York and New Jersey residents.

Wayside Gardens
Hodges, South Carolina 29695
Catalog is $1.00. A good selection of popular grasses.

White Flower Farm
Litchfield, Connecticut 06759
Catalog is $4.00, beautifully done. A few grasses and the beautiful *Hakonechlora macro albo-aurea variegata*. Also, the infamous Russian Buffalo Grass (*Hierochloe australis*).

The Wild Garden
Box 487
Bothell, Washington 98011
Catalog is $1.00. The tone is literate, the grasses are varied, and the Japanese sedges are unique.

Wildlife Nurseries
P. O. Box 2724
Oshkosh, Wisconsin 54901
List is free. They are the only major supplier of wild rice that I have found.

Wilson Seed Farms
Route 1, Box 7
Polk, Nebraska 68654
Free listing of prairie grasses and publishers of a beautiful book on the western grasslands: *Grass Land.*

Windrift Prairie Shop & Nursery
RD 2
Oregon, Illinois 61061
Free listing on extensive supply of native American grasses.

World Wide Seeds
J. L. Hudson, Seedsman
P. O. Box 1058
Redwood City, California 94064
Catalog is 50¢ and contains many seed offerings of grasses.

APPENDIX B: Garden Societies

The following societies all sponsor seed exchanges for members, and in every selection offered there are always grasses, sedges, and some bamboos. Their magazines or journals are literate, professional in every sense of the word, and well worth your time and attention.

Alpine Garden Society
Lye End Link, St. John's
Woking GU21 1SW
Surrey, England
Four bulletins per year; seed exchange in January; publishes many valuable booklets and monographs; $8.00 per year.

American Horticultural Society
7931 East Boulevard Drive
Alexandria, Virginia 22308
Six magazines per year; seed exchange in the spring; newsletter; $15.00 per year.

American Rock Garden Society
Mr. William T. Hirsh, Secretary
3 Salisbury Lane
Malvern, Pennsylvania 19355
Four bulletins per year; seed exchange in January; publishes many valuable booklets and monographs; $7.00 per year.

Scottish Rock Garden Club
R. H. D. Orr, C. A.
70 High Street, Haddington
East Lothian, Scotland
Two bulletins per year; seed exchange in the spring; $3.75 per year.

Wind-Chill Factor Chart

When planting many perennials, the gardener must remember the effect that wind has on the temperature. A calm 0°F is not bad at all, but with a 20 mph wind, it becomes an unbearable −39°. If such low temperatures bother you, they are equally disliked by many plants.

WIND-CHILL FACTOR

Temperature	Wind Speed								
	CALM	5	10	15	20	25	30	35	40
+50	50	48	40	36	32	30	28	27	26
+40	40	37	28	22	18	16	13	11	10
+30	30	27	16	9	4	0	−2	−4	−6
+20	20	16	4	−5	−10	−15	−18	−20	−21
+10	10	6	−9	−18	−25	−29	−33	−35	−37
0	0	−5	−21	−36	−39	−44	−48	−49	−53
−10	−10	−15	−33	−45	−53	−59	−63	−67	−69
−20	−20	−26	−46	−58	−67	−74	−79	−82	−85
−30	−30	−36	−58	−72	−82	−88	−94	−98	−100
−40	−40	−47	−70	−88	−96	−104	−109	−113	−116

CALM: Chimney smoke rises vertically.
1-12 mph: Leaves stir; you feel a breeze on your face.
13-24 mph: Branches stir; loose paper is blown about.
25-30 mph: Large branches move; wires whistle.
30-40 mph: Whole trees in motion; hard to walk against the wind.

APPENDIX D: Celsius - Fahrenheit Conversion

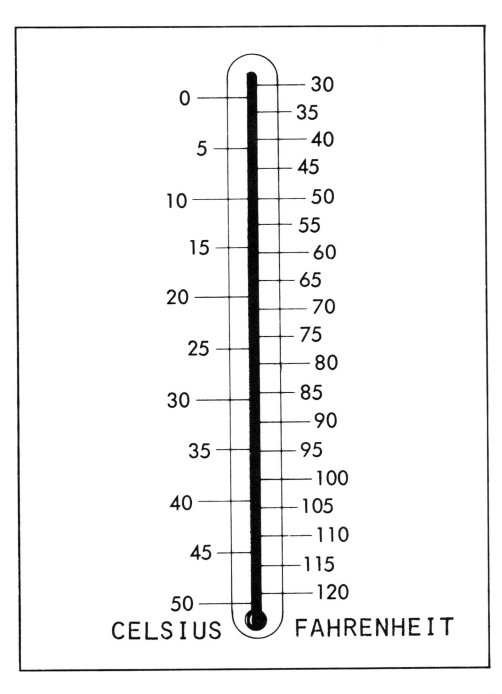

Bibliography

Agricultural Research Services of the United States Department of Agriculture. *Common Weeds of the United States.* New York: Dover Publications, 1971.
  Interesting to read, good illustrations, valuable maps on species distribution, but interest depends on your definition of a weed.
Bisset, Peter. *The Book of Water Gardening.* New York: A. T. De La Mare, 1907.
  A wonderful walk down Memory Lane; when water gardening was done primarily on estates.
Britton, Nathaniel Lord. *Manual of the Flora of the Northern States and Canada.* New York: Henry Holt and Company, 1905.
  An unillustrated checklist only for those with a passionate interest.
Britton, Nathaniel Lord, and Brown, Addison. *An Illustrated Flora of the Northern United States and Canada.* Vol. 1. 1913. New York: Dover Publications, 1970.
  No matter how many times you consult this work, it's still the best around. Most of the information is still valid.
Burton, Alfred. *Rush-Bearing.* Manchester: Brook and Chrystal, 1891.
  A well-written history of a colorful custom that has disappeared from the social science.
Clark, George H., and Fletcher, James. *Farm Weeds of Canada.* Ottawa: Ministry of Agriculture, 1909.
  Beautiful, color illustrations and nonscientific story of the battle between farmers and weeds.
Flint, Charles L. *A Practical Treatise of Grasses and Forage Plants.* New York: G. P. Putnam, 1857.
  Although much of the scientific information on agriculture is out of date, it still contains valuable information on grasses with beautiful, old illustrations.
Frederick, William H., Jr. *100 Great Garden Plants.* New York: Alfred A. Knopf, 1975.
  Good color pictures and descriptions of a few grasses and bamboos. Best for the gardener with some acreage.
Harkness, Bernard E. *The Seedlist Handbook,* 2nd edition. Bellona, N.Y.: Kashong Publications, 1976.
  A listing of all the plants in the seed exchanges of the American Rock Garden Society and a valuable checklist.
Hay, Roy, and Synge, Patrick M., *Color Dictionary of Flowers and Plants.* New York: Crown Publishers, 1975.
  A very valuable addition to any plant library, with hundreds of small but clear photos of perennial and annual flowers, including grasses.

Hortus Third. New York: Macmillian Company, 1976.

>The monumental revision of L. H. Bailey and Ethel Zöe Bailey's original work of nomenclature for the American Gardener, overseen by the staff of the L. H. Bailey Hortorium at Cornell University. An expensive but worthy addition to every gardener's library.

Hostek, Albert. *Native and Near Native Plants.* Long Island, N.Y.: Environmental Centers of Setauket-Smithtown, 1976.

>A well-done local guide to Long Island beaches and their plantlife.

Hotchkiss, Neil. *Common Marsh, Underwater and Floating-Leaved Plants of the United States and Canada.* New York: Dover Publications, 1972.

>While covering many plant species, this is more for the naturalist than the gardener.

Huxley, Anthony, ed. *Garden Perennials and Water Plants.* New York: Macmillan Company, 1971.

>An excellent pocket guide with colorful illustrations. Some juggling of information is necessary since the book is English, but still worthwhile.

————. *Mountain Flowers.* New York: Macmillan Company, 1972.

>Attractively illustrated and thorough guide to alpine flowers, including many grasses.

McClure, F. A. *The Bamboos A Fresh Perspective.* Cambridge: Harvard University Press, 1976.

>A definitive and serious text on the history and cultivation of the bamboos.

Meyer, Mary Hockenberry. *Ornamental Grasses.* New York: Charles Scribner's Sons, 1975.

>Deals mainly with cultivated grasses and includes some valuable lists, but unfortunately for me, a great deal on dyeing grasses with brilliant colors.

Meyer, Mary Hockenberry, and Mower, Robert G. *Ornamental Grasses for Home and Garden.* Ithaca, N.Y.: Cornell University.

>A key to the common ornamentals.

Perry, Frances. *Water Gardening.* London: Country Life, 1947.

>Another friendly and chatty English book on gardening that contains much useful information and history on aquatic plants and grasses.

Pohl, R. W. *How to Know the Grasses.* Dubuque: William C. Brown, 1968.

>Like most of the Brown Nature Keys, this is an excellent field guide.

Prescott, G. W. *The Aquatic Plants.* Dubuque: William C. Brown, 1969.

>Another excellent Brown Nature Key.

Stokoe, W. J. *The Observer's Book of Grasses, Sedges, and Rushes.* London and New York: Frederick Warne.

>Like all the other books in this series, this is a quaint, charming, and knowledgeable book that only the English could produce.

Swindells, Philip. *A Guide to Water Gardening.* New York: Charles Scribner's Sons, 1975.

>An up-to-date survey on aquatic plants available today.

Transactions of the New York State Agricultural Society, Vol. XXIX, 1896. Albany: Argus Printers, 1870.

>A charming and valuable antique.

United States Department of Agriculture. *Grass: The Yearbook of Agriculture.* Washington: U. S. Government Printing Office, 1948.

>Very thorough, very thick, and very U.S.D.A.

Wilson, Jim and Alice. *Grass Land.* Polk, Neb.: Wide Skies Press, 1967.

>Imaginative photographs, poetic text; will make a convert of any reader to saving the prairies of America.

Index